SHADOWFOLDS

SHADOWFOLDS

Surprisingly Easy-to-Make
Geometric Designs in Fabric

JEFFREY RUTZKY AND CHRIS K. PALMER

KODANSHA INTERNATIONAL
New York | Tokyo | London

▶ *Dedicated to Shuzo Fujimoto-sensei*

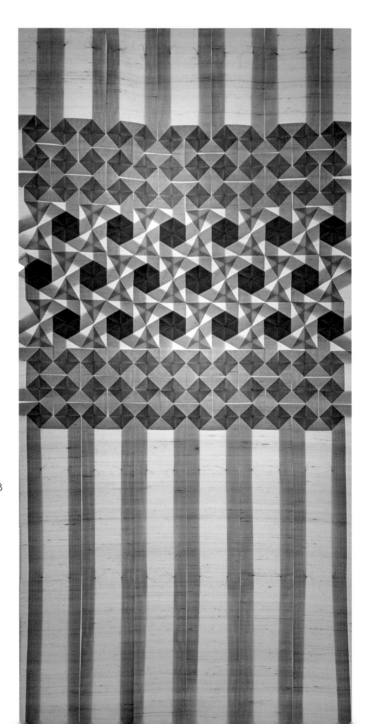

First published in North America in 2011 by

Kodansha America, LLC
451 Park Ave South
New York, New York 10016
United States

Kodansha International, Ltd.
1-17-14 Otowa
Bunkyo-ku, Tokyo 112-8652
Japan

Library of Congress Cataloging-in-Publication Data

Rutzky, Jeffrey.
    Shadowfolds : surprisingly easy-to-make geometric designs in fabric / by Jeffrey Rutzky and Chris K. Palmer.
        p. cm.
    Includes index.
    ISBN 978-1-56836-379-0
    1. Fabric folding. 2. Folds (Form) in art. I. Palmer, Chris K. II. Title
    TT840.F33R88 2011
    736'.98—dc22

                                        2010036978

Designed by Jeffrey Rutzky
Edited by Ruth O'Brien
Shadowfold photography by Mark A. Gore and Lynne Yeamans

Manufactured in Singapore by DNP America
10 9 8 7 6 5 4 3 2 1

CONTENTS

PREFACE

ALL OF THE ARTWORK I MAKE INVOLVES some form of geometry. Growing up, I enjoyed folding paper and making figures and compositions using origami. My interest grew in high school and college, with a focus on patterns and geometric design. George Bain's classic book *Celtic Art: The Methods of Construction* inspired me to draw and study traditional ornament.

After receiving my BFA, I traveled to Spain to visit Granada. I fell in love with the Alhambra and decided to live there for six months and study the tiling and elaborate mosaics left by the ancient Moors. I recorded these with hand drawings, learning to interpret the geometric language of the compositions.

I began to see ways to translate these patterns into folded paper. Examples by Tomoko Fuse inspired me to combine geometric tiling and origami. My first original compositions followed her approach of using flat unit origami of different shapes tiled together. I also wondered what it would be like to use cloth like it was paper, by starching it so it would fold similarly. Like a quilt, I fit folded cloth units together and sewed them into patterns I enjoyed.

When I was introduced to origami masters Robert Lang, Peter Engel, and Jeremy Shafer, they encouraged me to express the tilings I was studying by using a single sheet of paper. With the aid of some complex geometry, I began to understand how these repetitive patterns, known as tessellations, could be folded with one sheet.

In Japan, another origami master, Shuzo Fujimoto, was already doing this. I was so impressed with his work, I began to study the way he interpreted folds in a crease pattern. From photographs of Fujimoto's work, I learned his techniques for expressing tilings. My friendship with Jeremy Shafer led to work we created together, incorporating the tessellation principles I studied in the Alhambra.

At a conference in New York City, I met Tomoko Fuse, Jun Maekawa, and Toshikazu Kawasaki. They invited me to Japan to present my work and to meet Fujimoto-sensei. His encouragement was profound, and I was grateful to have his blessing as I continued to explore his art.

I returned to my interest in using textiles for these folded works, and explored the best techniques to achieve them. I stumbled a few times while figuring out how to efficiently make such complex patterns easy to produce. Once again, I tried using starch to treat the single sheet of cloth like paper, but it was still as difficult to fold. I finally discovered a simple way of bringing common points together to create patterns without difficult manipulation. The secret was to not think of the cloth as if it were paper.

This book shares my remarkable experience of developing a technique for surprisingly easy-to-make geometric designs in fabric.

—Chris K. Palmer

▼ *While studying in Granada from 1990 to 1991, I lived in a cave on this hillside at Sacremonte.*

OVERVIEW

► WHAT ARE SHADOWFOLDS?

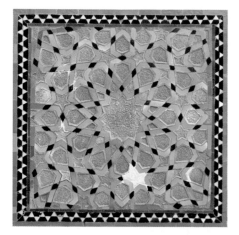

▲ *Ancient mosaic from Iran, translated into a Shadowfold.*

► *Preliminary drawing of underlying pattern.*

Shadowfolds are works of art created by folding cloth in patterns based on classic geometric designs. The patterns, taken from traditional architecture and the interior decorations of many cultures and periods, are given an added complexity due to the way the fabric and folds interact with light. Because these geometric patterns are usually found in tiles, to make them in cloth, as Shadowfolds, lends them a soft, warm appeal. By blending traditional patterns with a contemporary style, Shadowfolds evoke a timelessness while also creating a sense of exciting innovation.

PATTERN

Patterns contain elements in sets. A motif contained in an area known as the fundamental region (shown below) is copied and placed side-by-side to cover a surface.

TESSELLATION

The motif can be a wide variety of design elements. A special kind of motif composed of shapes placed together without gaps is called a tessellation. Familiar examples include many ancient patterns used to ornament walls, floors, and ceilings. Squares sewn together, like patches for a quilt, also form a tessellation. Tile mosaics, in particular, are made from an astounding array of shapes fitted together to form a composition. Although tessellations can have curved edges, patterns being designed with folded pleats are made of shapes with straight sides. These polygons then fit together to fill an area.

TESSELLATIONS AND TRADITIONAL CRAFT

Many forms of art use pattern and tessellation to decorate and ornament, often expressing a particular style for a certain geographic region or culture. For example, rings that have repeating motifs decorate Asian pottery; Middle Eastern cultures lay thousands of ceramic tiles to assemble vast mosaics; and American quilts are often pieced together with blocks of cut cloth. The patterns also have a particular expression that is unique to each medium, based on the properties of the material, as well as the construction techniques.

Cultures throughout history use tessellations in architecture and craft. Some of the best examples of repeating

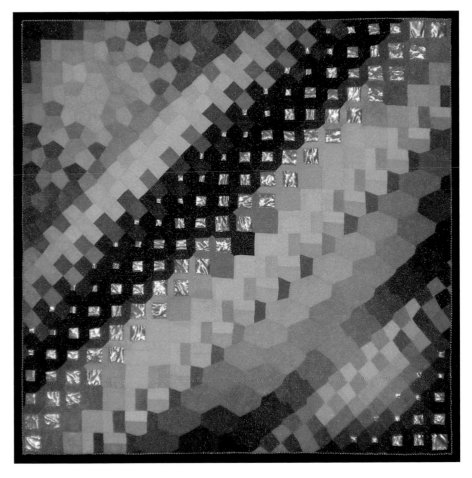

► *Tiled Torus with Changing Tiles* by Elaine Ellison, pieced cloth quilt, 44½ × 44½ inches, 2009.

▲ *Tiled mosaic, the Alhambra, c. 1300 BCE*

▲ *Punched panels, the Alhambra, c. 1300 BCE*

patterns are found in mosques and palaces built in the Middle East and in southern Spain, in a region known as Andalucía. Master builders make liberal use of mosaic ornament when decorating. These include walls, ceilings, panels, screens, doors, and pavements. Artisans make rugs, pottery, and other wares, such as cups, bowls, and platters using materials such as ceramic, wood, plaster, metal, stone, and textile.

THE ALHAMBRA

Andalucía is home to the city of Granada and the famous palace, the Alhambra. Built by the Moors in the 14th century, it contains some of the world's best examples of traditional tiling. The Alhambra is one of the most visited architectural monuments in Europe. There are ornamental styles composed of floral motifs, straight-line polygons, and a blend of both. M.C. Escher visited here several times, and his famous tessellations were heavily inspired by the symmetry of the Alhambra's tiles.

▼ *Wood ceiling panels, the Alhambra, c. 1300 BCE*

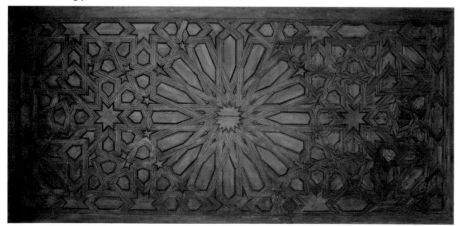

▼ *Plaster motifs, the Alhambra, c. 1300 BCE*

SOME PROPERTIES OF GEOMETRIC TESSELLATIONS

A surface with tiles that repeat is composed of two distinct parts: lines and vertices. There are an infinite number of ways to express a line. Lines made with wood shapes will be different than lines made by folding paper. The ends of each line meet to form a vertex. A vertex in plaster will be different than pieces sewn together from cut cloth. The composition of connected lines and vertices cover a surface. A surface pattern made from ceramic tiles, for example, is opaque. However, the same underlying pattern can be translucent when folded from paper or cloth.

Translucency is the unique property that makes a Shadowfolds pattern markedly different than in other mediums. When lines in a pattern are folded as pleats, the resultant shapes formed by the pleats become part of the artistic expression of the material. Tessellations folded this way in paper are a type of origami that is increasingly popular, though paper remains very difficult to fold this intricately.

Pictured below are some ways artisans have expressed lines, vertices, and patterns, in six different mediums. The first row shows examples of lines. Grooves in plaster and wood can look very similar; however, others, like the tile and stone look very different.

When a line is expressed by pleats in paper or cloth, several thicknesses produce a shadow when light passes through. The second row shows lines that meet at a vertex. A structure forms determined by the geometry of the intersection. When pleats in paper or cloth are made, these structures can expand to a greater variety of complex and beautiful forms. The third row shows tiling of lines and vertices making symmetrical forms. Some lines of symmetry spiral around a point and others are mirrored.

▼ *Ancient wood* ▼ *Ancient tile* ▼ *Ancient plaster* ▼ *Ancient stone* ▼ *Cloth quilt* ▼ *Pleated paper*

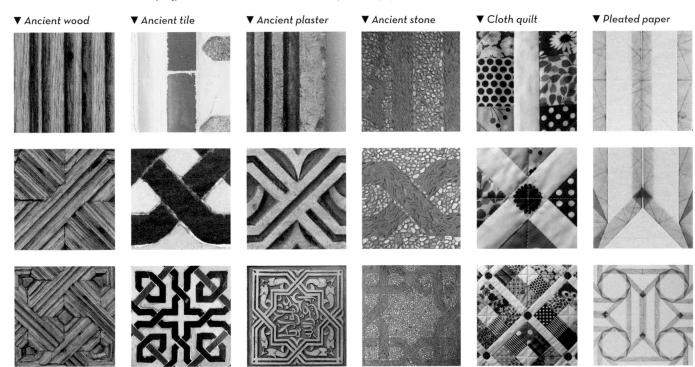

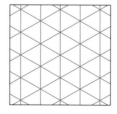

► *Palmer presented Fujimoto-sensei with a Shadowfold gift that replicates the pleated paper pattern on the cover of Fujimoto's book.*

THE FATHER OF PLEATED PAPER TESSELLATIONS

Shuzo Fujimoto is one of the foremost masters of origami and pioneered the technique of folding a single sheet of paper into a pleated tessellation. Born in Japan, Fujimoto began designing tessellations in a style known as *hira-ori,* or flat-fold. His work has a distinctive look that is classically Japanese, primarily using motifs made from hexagons, squares, and triangles. The underlying geometric pattern is a traditional tiling that has no known origin, and has been used across many cultures.

GRIDS, PLEATS, AND TWISTS

The method of folding these patterns in paper that Fujimoto developed often involved pre-creasing a grid, usually square or triangular.

When folded pleats meet at a vertex, they will form a structure depending on what direction they are laid flat. If they are all laid in the same direction around a point, a twist is formed that will flatten into a polygonal shape. For example, a triangle forms when three pleats meet, a square forms when four pleats meet, and a hexagon forms when six pleats meet, and so on.

When designing a pattern, the direction in which the final pleats lie becomes not only a technical consideration, but also an artistic one. The geometry of the underlying pattern and aesthetic considerations will both factor into considering the variety of structures possible that can be formed at a given vertex.

▼ *Fujimoto begins with a hand drawing of a tiling. He makes notes to work out how the lines of the tiling will become arranged into pleats. In the pattern below he indicates which twists will be on the top or bottom.*

From this initial sketch a crease pattern is made. Mountain and Valley Folds are indicated and precreased into paper with the help of a triangular grid.

Finally, the paper is pushed together along the folds to make a pleated tessellation.

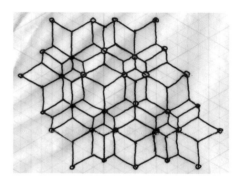

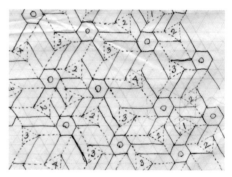

◄ *Square, hexagon, and triangle twists with lines and vertex.*

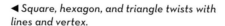

▼ *Most of Fujimoto's designs begin by using square or triangle gridlines as a base.*

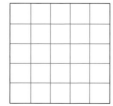

PAPER AS THE MEDIUM

To fold a tessellation using paper, a grid of small squares or triangles is generally creased in both directions. Alternating mountain and valley folds then need to be set, according to a crease pattern, so that a final collapse will be possible. Gentle coaxing of the newly oriented folds sometimes takes hours. This process can be immensely difficult, because as the surface distorts while collapsing and flattening individual pleats, there is always a risk of the paper splitting along the grid's folds, or at the corners that have many folds passing through them. Most designs require the constant folding and unfolding of pleats to finish each part of the pattern. Because the paper itself has a limited ability to distort, considerable stress is applied to these weakened areas.

CLOTH AS THE MEDIUM

Textiles have been used far longer than paper to fold pleats into artistic and functional expressions. Roman and Egyptian pleating were found in togas and ceremonial garments.

Tie-dye is a familiar technique used by many cultures whereby gathering cloth before immersing in pigments produces designs and patterns. A highly developed version of this tradition is the Japanese art of shibori.

▼ Early use of pleated fabric in a detail of a statue of the Emperor Hadrian in the Archaeological Museum of Olympia.

▼ Example of shibori made by pleating sections, then securing before dyeing. Different types of shibori produce varying results, depending on how the sections are secured, often with stitches. Also known as shaped-resist dyeing.

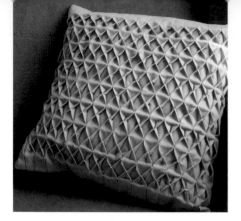

◄ Traditional smocking can create geometric patterns by sewing pleats together.

In the European method of smocking, gathering pleats in textiles is accomplished by pulling points together with threads. The majority of patterns in smocking use accordion pleats and then embroider decorative designs on top, popular in children's dresses. A few exceptional patterns, such as the Canadian weave, involve tying groups of points together to create intersections of pleats.

FOLDING COMPLEX PATTERNS IN CLOTH

Woven cloth's fibers are able to move more freely than paper's fibers. The most highly developed examples of pleated cloth were made in the past century by French artisans utilizing a sandwich mold. This method uses pairs of folded cardboard tessellations on each side of the cloth. When the cardboard molds are collapsed, the cloth is forced to take on the folds of the outside layers. This bundle is then heated to set the pattern in the cloth. The molds are then unfolded and the cloth retains a pleated pattern that can

then be used in a variety of applications. Sometimes the pleats are topstitched to hold them in place, or left loose to contract and expand. The molds can be used a limited number of times before they wear out.

The ability of cloth to distort easily makes it an ideal medium to fold intricate, yet surprisingly easy-to-produce tessellations. In a stark contrast to the sandwich method, a Shadowfold tessellation is made by tying points together, almost as easily as tying a shoelace. This method is not possible using paper.

▲ In this example of flower smocking, beads are added to points where the threads pull the fabric together.

▶ Gérard Lognon's workshop in Paris sandwiches fabric between cardboard molds and heats until folds are set.

EXAMPLES OF SIMPLE PLEATS AND TWISTS IN CLOTH

When points on a line or shape are pulled together, tied, and knotted, the resulting gathering will flatten into a pleat on the other side.

Anatomy of Pleats and Twists

This simple pleat is formed by folding the left line over the right line.

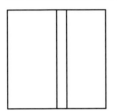

This octagonal twist is formed by pleating the lines over each other in a clockwise direction. The number of lines that make a vertex equal the number of sides a polygon twist will have. Below is the completed twist shown from the front and back.

▲ *Front of twist*   ▲ *Back of twist*

TRANSLUCENCY OF CLOTH

One of the great artistic aspects of pleated fabric is the ability to transmit light. A thin, light-colored fabric, when folded, will allow light to shine through at varying levels, depending on how many layers the pleats make. The amount of translucency also depends on the density of the weave and color. Tessellations, and even simple twists, are unusually beautiful because there are several "views" to be seen within a given pattern. The name Shadowfolds is derived from this property.

Many Shadowfolds have four distinct views:

- the front's opaque pattern
- the back's opaque pattern
- the front's translucent pattern
- the back's translucent pattern

The first two views are obvious: pleated folds on top, and the tiles sewn together on the back. However, it's the translucent views that reveal a hidden pattern, and it is usually different when viewed from either side.

The Four Views of a Shadowfold

 ▲ *Front opaque*   ▼ *Front translucent*   ▲ *Back opaque*   ▼ *Back translucent*

▶ APPLICATIONS FOR SHADOWFOLDS

PLEATS + TRANSLUCENCY = SHADOWFOLDS

The beautiful patterns of medieval mosaics and modern geometric tiling are the underlying structures of Shadowfolds. The flexible property of cloth allows pleats to be folded to augment and give a dimensionality not present in a flat tile surface. The translucent quality brings the geometric pattern and folded textile to a new level.

The possibilities of using Shadowfolds in design are limitless. Some applications will take advantage of light shining through and others will show the richness of folds that have a depth all their own. Room dividers and screens are two of the best ways to display Shadowfolds that have four distinct views. Window treatments will highlight the different views: a translucent view during the day and an opaque view

at night. A tablecloth, centerpiece, or bedspread is a good application for Shadowfolds that are primarily rich in texture on the front.

Pleated cloth is a popular style and when prepared panels are sewn into fashion, Shadowfolds add a tactile dimensionality. Accessories like purses, hats, and shoes can utilize ornamental Shadowfolds, making a design really stand out.

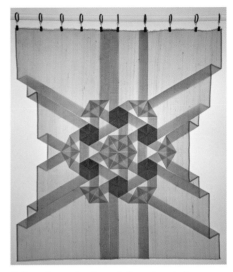

TRANSLUCENT APPLICATIONS

- **Window hangings** — display between glass or acrylic, with or without a frame
- **Window treatments, such as valances, and even curtains** — patterns can be easily repeated for covering large areas
- **Screens and room dividers** — panels constructed like Shoji screens, or windows between rooms and breezeways
- **Lampshades and light boxes** — alternate views by flipping a switch

OPAQUE APPLICATIONS

- **Wall hangings** — suspend from a rod, or mount in a frame
- **Tablecloths** — display under protective glass
- **Centerpieces and runners** — bring a contemporary look to doilies
- **Book covers** — quickly craft small panels onto special albums
- **Bedspreads, quilts, and pillow shams** — large or small patterns add dimension to a room
- **Fashion** — sew panels into all types of garments, handbags, ties, and hats

◄◄ A long strip of dodecagon whirl spool twists makes a beautiful valence in a downtown office.

► This version of Pinwheel Path is hung in the window using a simple acrylic frame.

▲ By using a simple curtain rod and clips you can easily change the Shadowfolds on display.

▼ Wrapping a lampshade is a warm way to display Shadowfolds.

► FOLDS AND FASHION

Shadowfolds will undoubtedly have a special place in fashion, especially haute couture. Many designers have incorporated pleats and folds into their work. Some are very complex and can only be produced in specialized shops or with machines. Mariano Fortuny and Issey Miyake created a variety of sophisticated pleating techniques and used them to produce stunning designs. Miyake continues to make a specialized line of folded fashion called Pleats Please.

Origami folds are popular accents for modern fashion. One multi-disciplined artist, Polly Verity, makes garments entirely from folded paper.

One innovative designer, however, creatively integrated Shadowfolds in his line of haute couture. David Rodriguez, in New York, requested various elements to be made, such as an ornamental flower or a tessellated panel, which were then sewn into a finished garment. Rodriguez's choice of fabrics, including satin, toile, wool, and even leather, displayed a variety of ways to use Shadowfolds in fashion.

▼ *UK artist Polly Verity uses curves and corrugations to make fashion from folded paper.*

▼ *Renowned Japanese designer Issey Miyake's 1994 Flying Saucer dress pays homage to Noguchi's paper lanterns.*

▼ *Spanish designer Mariano Fortuny created this Grecian-style pleated silk gown in 1907. A Delphos dress has been called "a poem in pleats." Fortuny also patented a silk-pleating machine in 1909.*

▶ *SoHo Partnership's 1998 fashion show in New York City featured American designer David Rodriguez, who incorporated a variety of Shadowfold designs in his couture.*

▼ *Neckline detail of nine-sided star flower with radiating pleats in toile; frontpiece of cotton jacket with pentagon and hexagon stars; radiating rosette sewn into front of toile and cotton dress.*

► HOW TO MAKE SHADOWFOLDS

SEW FOLDING BASICS

The technique developed to make Shadowfolds is surprisingly easy. Simply connect dots with a needle and thread, and the spaces in between the dots create pleats and twists. Once a group of knots are tied on the back, the front is ready to fold. Detailed instructions and tips for each step are in the next section, however, the basic steps are:

1 Transfer a dot pattern to the fabric.
2 Sew adjacent points together.
3 Flatten resulting pleats and twists.

Transferring the Pattern

There are just a few tools needed to help transfer the patterns in this book to a piece of fabric. The basic steps are:

1 Enlarge the pattern to the required size using a photocopier or scanner.
2 Tape the printed pages together to complete the pattern.
3 Punch holes at each dot using a hand punch or other paper drill.
4 Tape or pin the pattern to the back of the fabric.

5 Mark each dot using a colored pencil.
6 Remove the paper pattern and double-check that each dot is clearly marked.
7 Use a pencil to lightly connect the dots, with the printed pattern as a guide.

Sewing the Dots Together

The only things needed to sew the folds are a needle and thread. The basic steps are:

1 On the back of the fabric, pick up just a few threads with the needle across each dot.
2 Connect the adjacent dots, either in a clockwise or counterclockwise direction.
3 Tie an overhand knot and gently pull the thread ends together to gather all the dots to one point.
4 Finish by tying a couple of overhand knots to secure.
5 Trim the threads, leaving about ½ inch (1 cm).

Flattening the Pleats and Twists

To finish some of the projects in this book, it will be helpful to have a sewing machine. An iron is also used to flatten some of the pleats to the edges of the fabric. The basic steps are:

1 With your hands, flatten the pleats and twists on the front side to form the Shadowfold.
2 Use a cool iron to help press the pleats and twists, if desired.
3 Use a warm iron without steam to evenly press the edge pleats.

The edges of the Shadowfold will be finished differently depending on the project. If the Shadowfold is to be displayed separately, then the edge could be hemmed or serged before folding. In some designs, it may be desirable to serge and trim the pleated edge. Plan the initial size of the fabric for the desired result. When incorporating the Shadowfold into a subsequent design, it can be treated like any single fabric piece.

▼ *Print, punch, and transfer the pattern.*

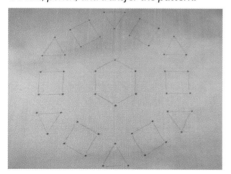

▼ *Sew the dots together.*

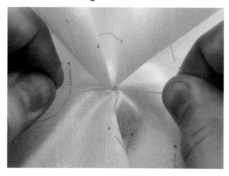

▼ *Flatten the pleats and twists.*

SHADOWFOLD SECRETS

Tips for techniques on each project, or general tips that will help to make Shadowfolds easier, are shown throughout the book in this box.

TECHNIQUES FOR PLANNING SHADOWFOLDS

Before cutting fabric or transferring a pattern, begin by thinking about how the final piece will be used. How big will it be after pleating? How much border should it have? Should the edge be serged or hemmed, before or after pleating?

Each project in this book will specify the amount of fabric needed and the size of the finished piece. These measurements will be approximate for the percentage of enlargement of each pattern. Beginners should try making Shadowfolds at the given sizes, but many projects can be customized.

Radiating and Converging Edge Pleats

In some Shadowfold designs, the edge pleats extend or radiate endlessly from the outermost twists in the pattern. For other designs, the edge pleats converge where they would resolve in another twist, continuing the tessellation pattern indefinitely.

Radiating pleats add additional flexibility to "frame" the tessellation. See *Watering Fujimoto's Garden* on page 32. Compose the Shadowfold with the

▲ *Resist fussing with the twists and pleats on the front side until all knots are tied on the back.*

surrounding edge pleats in a way that best suits a particular pattern or project.

Converging pleats end where they cross, sometimes a short distance from the outermost twists. See *Pinwheel Path* on page 68. The edge can be serged or hemmed, or make a seam when sewn onto another piece of fabric. Making

a plain border can dramatically set off opaque Shadowfolds.

TECHNIQUES FOR TRANSFERRING PATTERNS

The patterns in this book are intended to be photocopied, scanned, or downloaded, so that they can be enlarged to

▼ *Shadowfolds with radiating pleats in all directions can have a variable margin from the tessellation to the finished edge.*

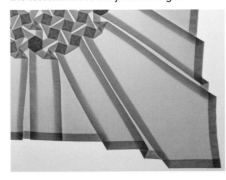

▼ *Shadowfolds with pleats that converge are part of the next twist in the tessellation and must be finished before they "crash."*

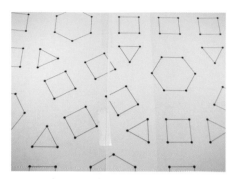

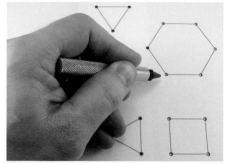

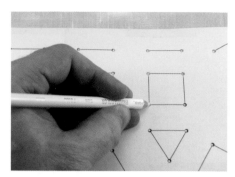

▲ Tape the printed pattern together.

▲ Punch the holes in the pattern.

▲ Mark the dots on the fabric.

the appropriate size. Some of the patterns will be a section of the full design, which can be tiled, rotated around a central point, or mirrored onto the fabric itself. Each project will illustrate any steps necessary to tile the pattern.

Enlarging the Pattern Using a Photocopier

Set the photocopier to the percentage given on the pattern. Use the largest paper size available (usually 11×17 inches or A3). Be certain that the page is flat to avoid any optical distortion. Move the page on the copier's glass to make overlapping enlargements that show the entire dot pattern.

Downloading the Pattern as a PDF File

For your convenience, the patterns can be downloaded as a PDF file from www.shadowfolds.com/bookpatterns.

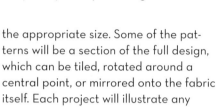

▶ Patterns can be tiled, rotated around a central point, or mirrored.

With the free Acrobat Reader software (www.adobe.com), print the file's pages at 100% since they are already enlarged.

Taping the Printed Pages Together

Lay out all of the pages onto a work surface in the correct order. Refer to the entire pattern to help. Tape together the centermost and its adjacent page, aligning repeated dots carefully onto one another. Finish piecing the remaining pages until the full pattern is complete. Trim any large overlapping pages from the back.

Punching Holes

Place the pattern onto a cutting mat to protect the work surface. Use a 3/32–1/8-inch (2–3 mm) hand punch or other paper drill to make a hole at each dot. Craft paper punches or drills for use with eyelets for scrapbooking are ideal.

Cutting and Preparing the Fabric

Refer to the section on *Techniques for Planning Shadowfolds* on page 23 to help decide how to treat the edge of the cut fabric. A straight-stitched, hand-rolled, ironed hem is a good treatment for one-piece Shadowfolds that are framed, hung or otherwise displayed as is. When using silk, it's convenient to serge the edge to prevent fraying, although not absolutely necessary.

Taping the Dot Pattern

On the backside of the fabric, position the pattern so it is centered as desired. Measure from the edge of the fabric to the outermost dots so the pattern is aligned evenly. Tape the pattern on all edges to secure.

Marking the Dots onto the Fabric

One of the best ways to mark the dot pattern onto the fabric is with a colored pencil. Use a white pencil to mark most fabrics. Even when marking light-colored silk, you can easily see the dot pattern. It may be preferable to use a darker color to mark some dark fabrics so that the dots won't be seen on the back after they are sewn

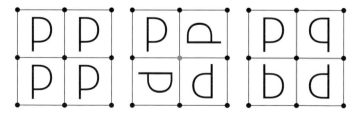

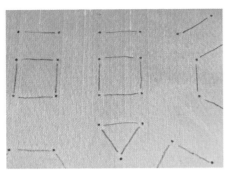

▲ *Mark the connecting dots to be tied together. Note: blue is used for clarity.*

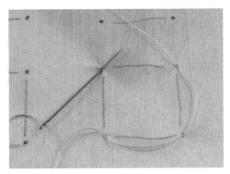

▲ *Sew the connecting dots together.*

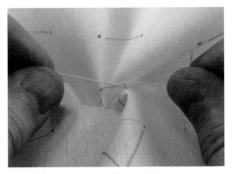

▲ *Pull the points together and knot.*

together. *Note: In the instructional photos, a blue pencil is used for clarity.* Practice marking dots on a swatch of the fabric used for the project. Make dots no larger than about 1/16 inch (1.5 mm).

Double-Checking the Dot Pattern

Once sew folding is underway and a number of knots are tied, it will be very difficult to add missing dots. *Double-check that each dot is clearly marked!* If any dots are missed after sew folding, untie a number of surrounding knots. Carefully align the paper pattern on that section, making sure the fabric is flat, and mark the missing dot.

Connecting the Dots

Especially for beginners, it is helpful to very lightly mark the connecting dots on the fabric, using the printed pattern as a guide. Use an ordinary pencil on light-colored fabrics and a white pencil on darker fabrics. Once the first group is tied, the fabric will no longer lie flat near the knot. The groups of dots to sew together may be more difficult to see, relative to one another. After some experience making Shadowfolds, it will be more intuitive to recognize the

pattern of shapes and eliminating this step will not lead to common mistakes.

TECHNIQUES FOR SEW FOLDING

The key to making Shadowfolds is the process of sew folding. By picking up each dot in sequence and tying the points, fabric is brought together, ready to be flattened as pleats and twists.

Picking Up the Points

Thread a small, fine needle with a single strand of topstitching thread, or a double strand of sew-all thread that matches the fabric's color. Always on the back of the fabric, look for a shape, such as a triangle, square, or hexagon, whose dots are connected. Pick up just a few threads with the needle across the first dot. Pull the thread through, leaving a few inches (8–10 cm) at the end. Connect the adjacent dots, either in a clockwise or counterclockwise direction, until the last dot is threaded.

Tying the Knots

Make an overhand knot between the first and last dot and gently pull the thread ends together to gather all the

dots to one point. Look for small folds of fabric that may be protruding from the back side and, if necessary, loosen the knot slightly and pull any folds fully to the front. Be sure the overhand knot is pulled tight enough to hold, but not too tight that the thread breaks. Secure the knot by tying two or three additional overhand knots to secure. The pucker of fabric should be tight, without any hole between the gathered points. If the gathered points are too loose, cut the knotted thread carefully and retie. Trim the threads, leaving about 1/2 inch (1 cm).

The order in which the knots are tied doesn't matter, as long as only the right groups of dots are tied together. However, it is helpful to follow a logical progression, such as from the center outwards, to help keep track of the groups of shapes. Notice the underlying pattern of polygons that develops, and tessellates, throughout the entire piece. If one of these shapes looks awkward or unsymmetrical, there may be a simple, easy-to-fix mistake.

Common Mistakes

One mistake often made by beginning sew folders is to connect the wrong dots

▶ *Spread the twist by laying all pleats around each sewn point in the same direction.*

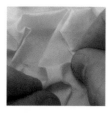

▶ *Flattened twists can spiral clockwise or counterclockwise.*

▶ *The first twist you make will inform the other shape's directions, and ripple throughout the tessellation.*

together, or to miss a dot as part of a shape, such as connecting only three dots for a square twist. Keeping an eye on the printed pattern helps identify the next group of dots to tie together. Another common mistake is not marking a dot from the punched paper pattern. This might go unnoticed until portions of the Shadowfold have been completed, making it difficult to re-mark since the fabric will not lie flat. It's best to untie several neighboring knots so the paper pattern can be realigned accurately, and the missing dot marked.

TECHNIQUES FOR FINISHING SHADOWFOLDS

When sew folding, resist the temptation to turn the piece over to begin flattening the pleats and twists until you've tied all the knots. There is an amazing "a-ha moment" once the dots are all tied together on the back, or at least a

section of the pattern that repeats, such as a central twist and its surrounding shapes. When the Shadowfold is turned over to the front, the puffed shapes and neighboring pleats are nearly ready to fold themselves.

Flattening the Pleats and Twists

All extra folded fabric that become pleats and twists will lie on the front side of the Shadowfold and flat, neat edges will form a regular pattern on the back.

Twists can form clockwise or counterclockwise spirals, and the pleats that radiate from them will lie flat on one side or the other. The first twist's direction will inform which side the radiating pleats will fold and in which direction the neighboring twists will form. There is no right or wrong way to begin; however, each project's instructions will match its accompanying photographs. Some projects have pleats

that form a mitered corner and must lie a specific way to form the Shadowfold pattern shown.

Making Pleats Straight and Neat

Begin by pulling up all of the pleats from the middle, between each of the twists. Lightly press a crease, from the middle running toward each end of the pleat.

Lightly press the puffed shape flat, making sure the underlying pleats are all lying flat in one direction. Where three pleats meet, there will be a triangle; four pleats, a square, and so on. Neaten all of the underlying fabric around the gathered points to produce a clean, crisp shape on top.

Continue lightly pressing pleats throughout the design. No pleat will fold over itself. If this happens, a neighboring twist is flattening in the wrong direction. Just reverse the twist's direction so the pleats lie flat.

▼ *After tying the knots, the back of the Shadowfold will look neat, symmetrical, and lie completely flat.*

▼ *The front will have a series of puffy folds and edges ready to shape into twists and pleats.*

▼ *Begin shaping by picking up pleats between twists and gently crease with your fingers.*

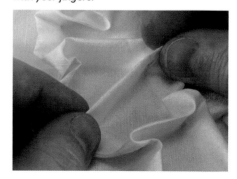

▶*All pleats will lie flat if twists spiral in the correct direction. Reverse any twists to fix connecting pleats that still stand up.*

A cool iron can help flatten pleats, but use caution to avoid removing too much of the dimensional texture. The twisted shapes often look better when they're not too crisp.

Flattening Edge Pleats

First use a cool iron to help extend outer pleats neatly to the edge of the fabric. Then apply a warm, dry iron on the edges only, to keep the pleat's shape and make the whole Shadowfold's border even and symmetrical. Creasing the edges will also make additional serging or hemming of the edge easier.

The Finished Shadowfold

If the edge still needs to be hemmed or serged, pin the edge pleats to hold them flat and straight.

Hold the finished Shadowfold to the light and admire the different patterns formed from the front and back.

▼ *Gently flatten twists by arranging all radiating pleats in the same direction. Continue with the neighboring twists.*

▣◀ *A short video demonstrating the basic sew folding steps can be seen at www.shadowfolds.com/videotutorial*

FINDING FABRIC

A variety of fabrics can be used to make Shadowfolds. Finding the right type will depend on several factors:

- the desired translucency
- the scale of the finished piece
- the pattern's complexity
- the width of the final pleats
- the intended application

Many of the Shadowfolds shown in the *Gallery* chapter of this book were made from dupioni silk. The projects in this book will specify a type of fabric to best achieve the application shown. A list of reliable fabric sources can be found in the *Resources* section on page 123.

These are some recommended fabrics used to make Shadowfolds. Colors are available in the various types of fabrics; however, avoid dying since washing will remove the sizing used for stiffness. At least for beginners, crisp, thin, and strong fabrics help make the pleats and twists easier to set into their final patterns.

- **Dupioni silk** is the most common silk used for bridal gowns. Dupioni has a stiff feel that will hold a crease well, yet resists wrinkling. It has a dull luster and there are some lumpy, horizontal lines, called "slubs," that add a random texture.

- **Shantung silk** originated from China and is also referred to as raw silk. Shantung has a tighter weave and will give a bit less translucency. The texture is similar to dupioni. Shantung silk is springy and hard to fold in one direction due to the weave structure; challenging to use unless experienced in making Shadowfolds.
- **Taffeta silk** is tightly woven, smooth on both sides, and shiny. It is stiff, but will have less translucency, especially with darker colors. Many colors are available, including iridescent. Taffeta also is made from rayon, cotton, and acetate. Natural or synthetic taffetas are great for opaque Shadowfold applications.
- **Satin** has a glossy surface and a dull back. It is very smooth and not normally stiff. Satin is good for opaque applications where a soft fold is desired. Make sure the pleats and twists are not too small since it is too thick to form fine detail.
- **Cotton** comes in a wide variety of colors and will hold a crease well. It is not as translucent or strong as silk, but is less expensive.
- **Linen** comes from a plant fiber like cotton, has a much stiffer feel, and holds a crease very well. It is not as translucent, but it is as strong as silk, and good for opaque applications.
- **Muslin** is a loosely woven cotton widely used by dressmakers to test designs for fit, and is inexpensive. It is very translucent and great for practicing with Shadowfolds.

- **Toile** and **organza** are very lightweight, sheer fabrics. For Shadowfolds, they would best be used in applications where maximum translucency is desired. These fabrics may be manageable after some experience.
- **Jersey, knit,** or other **stretch fabrics** are *not recommended* for making Shadowfolds. They do not hold a crease well, fold differently along the bias, and will distort the polygonal shapes and tessellation pattern.
- **Patterned fabrics** are also not recommended for making Shadowfolds. The fabric's grain direction shifts continually throughout every tessellation, and thus would conflict with the patterns of the Shadowfold.
- **Leather, suede,** and **felt** could be used to make simple, opaque patterns that would be subsequently sewn in to accent a fashion accessory or similar application. Because they are so thick, experimenting with these materials require experience making Shadowfolds.

▼ *Patterned fabric can interfere with the Shadowfold's geometric structure. Leather has many possibilities to explore.*

SHADOWFOLDS CARE

The best way to protect Shadowfolds made for display is to frame them between sheets of glass or acrylic. This prevents dust and other contaminants from soiling the fabric itself. Here are a few more tips:

- **UV protection** — It's best to hang Shadowfolds in windows that receive indirect light. Fading can occur with all fabrics and some protection is afforded by using UV-resistant glass or acrylic when framing.
- **Cleaning** — Spot-clean only with a solvent appropriate for the fabric. Silk can show water spots easily. Dry cleaning or washing is not recommended, since agitation will likely loosen knots and unfold the Shadowfold.
- **Dusting** — Twirl a feather duster lightly to clean exposed Shadowfolds. Do not rub, since this can force dust particles to embed in the fabric's fibers.

▼ *This Shadowfold hung in a southern window for years without UV protection. The silk has become brittle and is easily cracked.*

◄ *Sandwiching acrylic pieces is an elegantly simple way to display Shadowfolds in a window.*

▼ *Simple suction cups can be used with invisible thread to hang small Shadowfolds in the window or on many other surfaces.*

DISPLAYING SHADOWFOLDS

There are endless applications for Shadowfolds in design and fashion. Finding a way to display any given project will also be a creative endeavor. Here are a few ideas that will take advantage of any hidden patterns in a translucent Shadowfold or the richness of the folded form in an opaque one.

Using Suction Cups

Small and lightweight Shadowfolds can be easily hung in a window with two or more suction cups. Affix loops of transparent thread or thin fishing line to the top corners of the finished piece to hang directly on the front side of the rubber cups. Wire hooks that come with some suction cups are not needed and detract from the simple mounting.

Framing in Glass or Acrylic

Any Shadowfold that you want to transmit light can be mounted between sheets of glass or acrylic. The entire piece can appear to float within the edges, with or without a frame. Custom-made hanging hardware can be found at specialty retailers or on the Internet. UV-resistant glass or acrylic is recommended for window settings.

The weight of the glass or acrylic panes will factor into what hardware is best. Acrylic has the advantage of being lightweight and crack-resistant, but can scratch easily and warp. Glass cleans well and will not warp, but is much heavier, especially in larger sizes.

In frameless applications with acrylic, it is easy to drill holes, with the proper bit, and use off-the-shelf hardware for mounting panes together. Glass presents greater challenges that should be solved by a professional.

A good framing shop will help envision the best way to display this work of art.

Hanging from a Rod

There are many choices of hardware for hanging Shadowfolds similar to curtains

- **Iron touch-up** — Use low heat without water or steam and a pillowcase on top to press creases again.
- **Sew-fold repair** — If any knots loosen, or a thread breaks, simply gather the same points again and make a new knot. Use an iron, as shown above, to re-crease, if necessary.
- **Storage** — Shadowfolds are easily stored rolled loosely in standard mailing tubes. For additional protection from humidity, before rolling, fit the Shadowfold inside a large plastic dry cleaning bag.

Shadowfolds are works of fine art and proper care will assure that they provide lasting beauty.

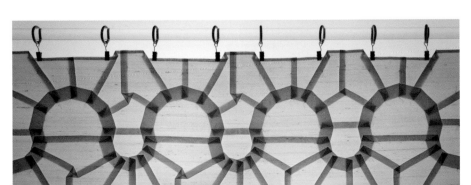

◄ *Hanging from a rod using curtain clips is an effective way to hang larger Shadowfolds, and makes it easy to change designs in a particular setting.*

or other draperies. This method is very practical for larger pieces. Affix loops of transparent thread or thin fishing line across the top edge in 1½–2 inch (4–5 cm) intervals and string across a rod. Another, even simpler method uses rings that have small clips designed for hanging any textile.

These applications have other advantages. One benefit is the ease of displaying different Shadowfolds from time to time in a limited space. One challenge to consider is the effect gravity will have on larger pleats. Placing additional knots along pleats that point up can mitigate this. If hanging with clips, rotating the Shadowfold can help as well, since most Shadowfolds are symmetrical.

SHADOWFOLD SECRETS

Some long pleats may need additional knots tied on their edges, in the middle, if they face up and sag a bit when the Shadowfold is hung vertically.

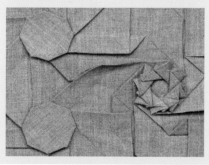

Valances

The ability of Shadowfolds to endlessly repeat a tessellation pattern makes them ideal for custom decorative treatments atop any size window.

Pillow Shams

Decorative covers for pillows are a great way to display Shadowfolds. Design by sewing the finished front panel to two overlapping pieces for the back, right sides together, then turn inside out. Use the same type of fabric or try a contrasting texture or color.

Light Boxes

A custom-made light box can frame Shadowfolds, with an instantaneous view revealing the hidden pattern. Smaller pieces could be displayed with retrofitted light boxes that photographers use for viewing negatives and transparencies. Larger backlit installations can be part of an overall interior design.

Lamps

Incorporate Shadowfolds into table or floor lamps, transforming them into sculptural works of art.

ENJOYING SHADOWFOLDS

The projects in this book are presented as a guide towards using your own creativity and ideas to create unique works of art. Once you are familiar with the fundamental techniques, you are encouraged to experiment with the patterns.

But most of all, you are encouraged to enjoy making Shadowfolds. When fine art is viewed in a gallery, the public is missing most of what is special about that object—how it was made. Understanding the process of making Shadowfolds is an art unto itself.

◀ *The dichotomy of a simple technique to produce a complex result is at the heart of creating Shadowfolds.*

▶▶ *Zillij Twelvefold,* folded silk, 1997. Detail of backlit view.

THE SHADOWFOLDS GALLERY DISPLAYS expanded versions of some of the projects in this book, as well as more advanced designs. Once you've mastered the techniques, you can glean ideas here to make larger Shadowfolds by repeating the dot patterns to make your own custom pieces.

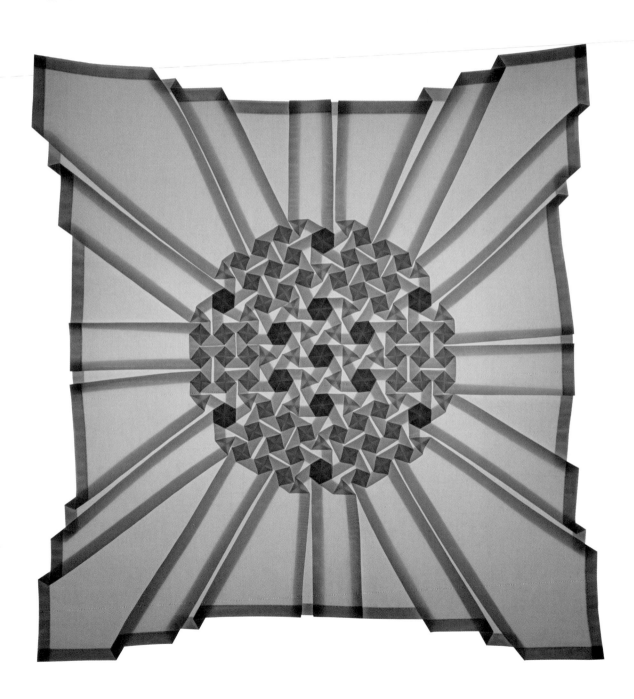

◄◄ *Watering Fujimoto's Garden*, folded silk, 19½ × 19½ inches, 2007. Front-lit (left) and backlit (right) views.

▼ *Zillij Tenfold*, folded silk, 60 × 36 inches, 1997. Front-lit view.
►► Backlit view.

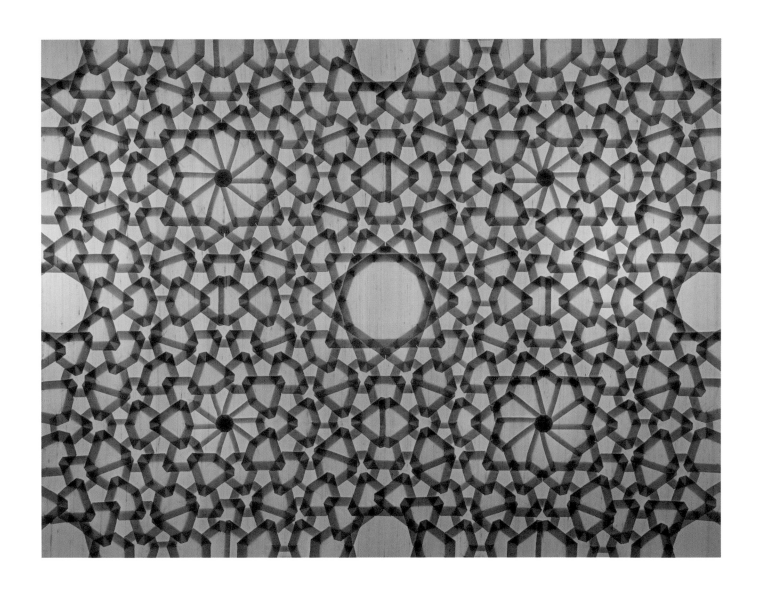

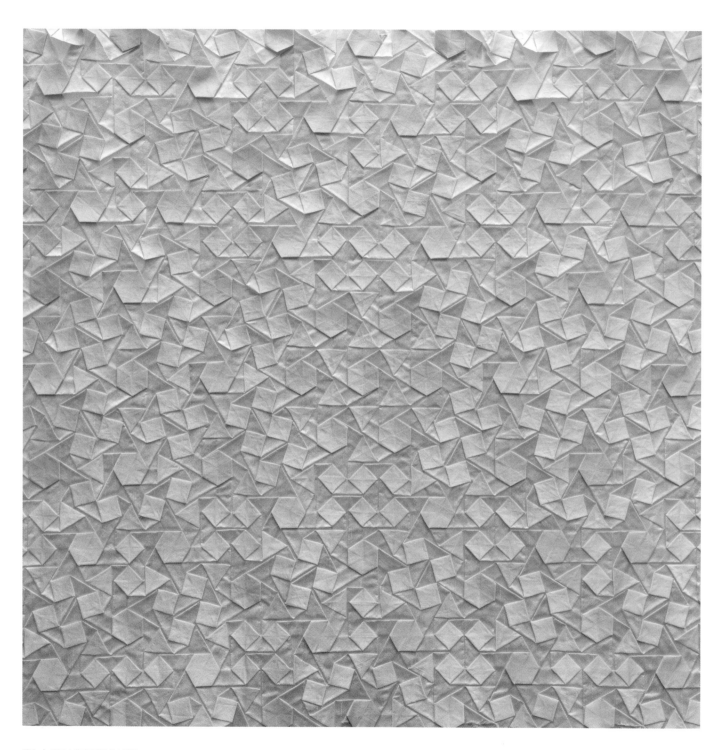

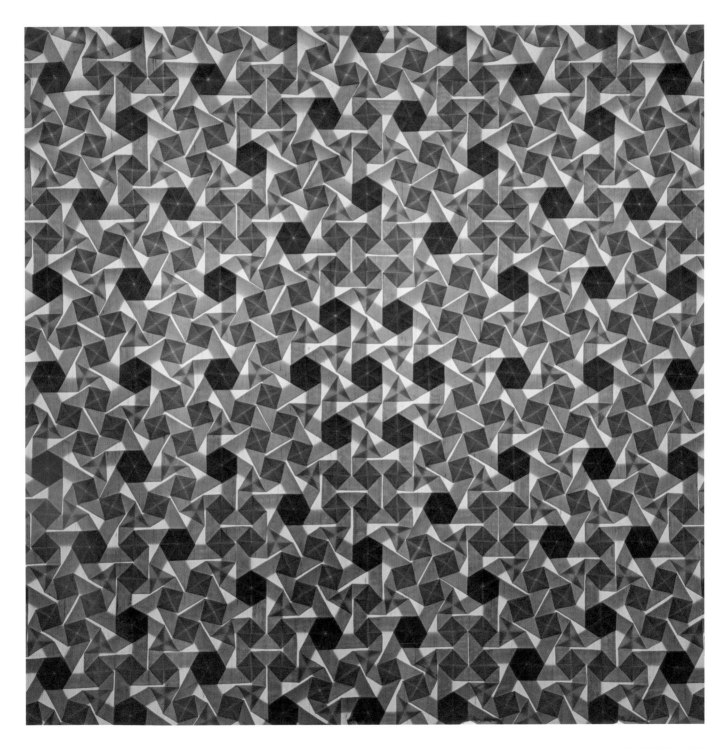

◄◄ *Pinwheel Path Extended,* folded silk, 36 × 36 inches, 1997. Front-lit (left) and backlit (right) views.

▶ *Zillij Eightfold,* folded cotton, 36 × 24 inches, 1997. Front-lit (top) and backlit (bottom) views.

▶▶ *Ring of Twist Octagons,* folded linen, 36 × 36 inches, 1996.

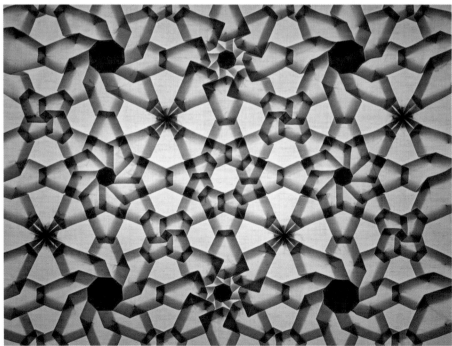

▶ *Decagon Scales,* folded cotton,
30 × 24 inches, 1996. Front-lit (top)
and backlit (bottom) views.

▶▶ *Variegated Scales,* folded silk,
36 × 24 inches, 1998.

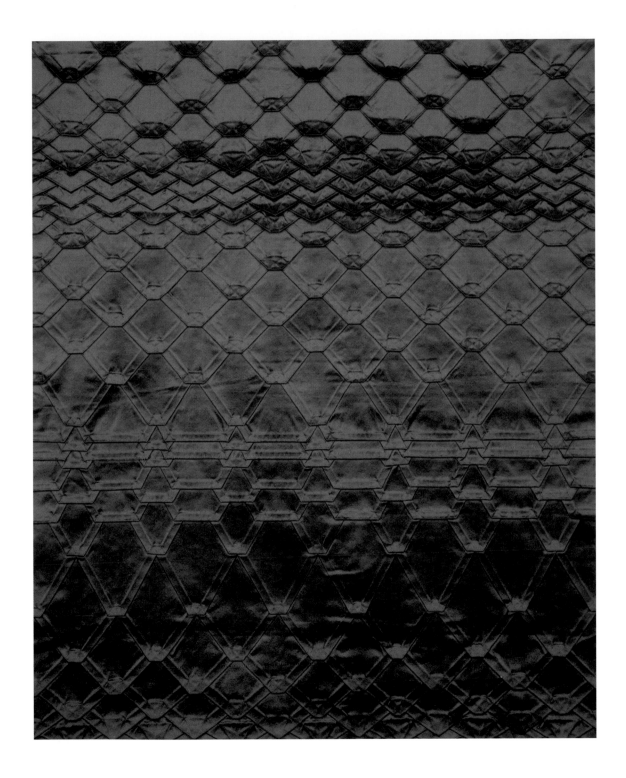

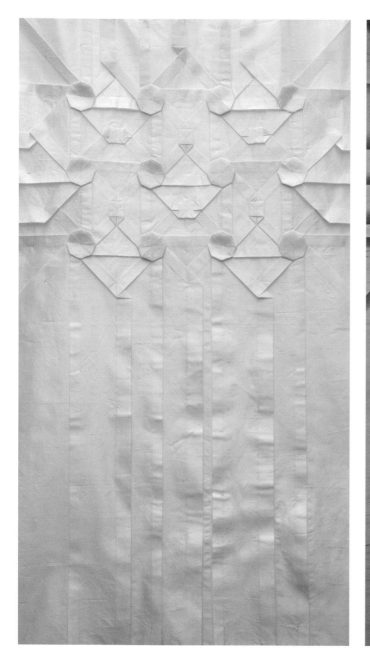

▼ *Twist Octagon Flag,* folded silk, 60 × 30 inches, 1997. Front-lit (left) and backlit (right) views.

▶▶ *Open-Back-Twist Octagons,* folded silk, 72 × 30 inches, 1998. Front-lit (top) and backlit (bottom) views.

▼ *Fujimoto's Flag*, folded cotton,
72 × 30 inches, 1997. Front-lit (left)
and backlit (right) views.

▶▶ *Zillij Twelvefold*, folded silk, 48 × 30
inches, 1997. Front-lit (top) and backlit
(bottom) views.

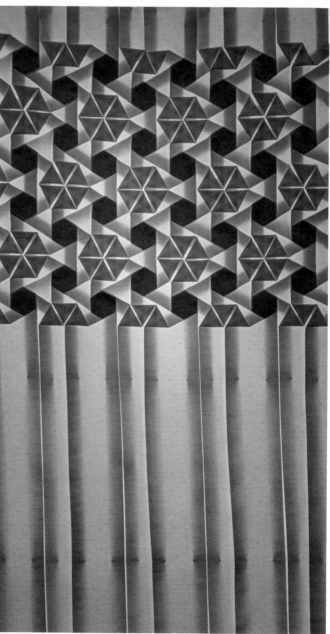

► *Stars of David,* folded silk, 48 × 30 inches, 1997. Front-lit (top) and backlit (bottom) views.

►► *Rosette Flag,* folded silk, 72 × 36 inches, 1997. Front-lit (left) and backlit (right) views.

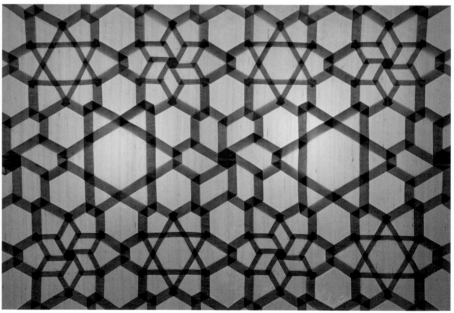

▲ *Waves,* folded silk, 36 × 16 inches, 1998.
Front-lit view.
▶▶ Backlit view.

▼ *Dodecagon Whirl Spools Banner,* folded silk,
72 × 15 inches, 1997. Front-lit view.
▶▶ Backlit view.

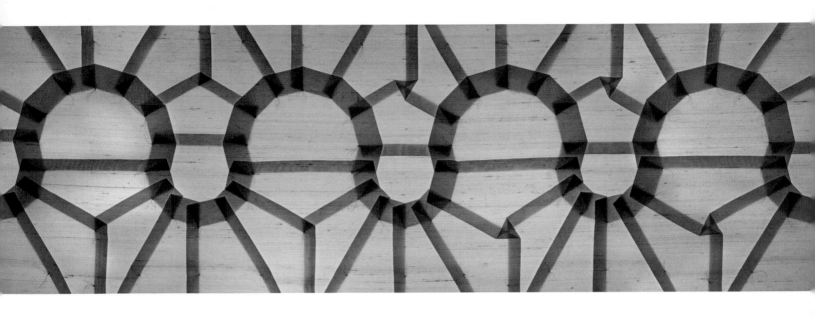

PROJECTS

PENTAGONAL STAR PILLOW

Difficulty: 🪡 | *Size:* **12 inches** (30 cm)
Fabric: **18 × 36 inches** (46 × 92 cm) **of silk**
Materials: **Needle, top-stitch thread, hand punch, pencil, iron, square ruler, pins, sewing machine**

START SEW-FOLDING SHADOWFOLDS WITH this simple Pentagonal Star Pillow. After tying just a few knots, this beautiful star virtually folds itself!

Prepare Cloth and Transfer Pattern

1 Cut the fabric into two 18×18 inch (46×46 cm) squares.
2 Enlarge the pattern on page 115 to 147% of original size, or download and print using the instructions on page 24.
3 Punch holes through the pattern at each marked circle.
4 Center pattern and tape to the fabric.
5 Mark each point using a pencil. *Double-check to be sure you've marked every point.* It's very hard to re-mark points once neighboring points are sewn together.
6 Remove the pattern and, using a pencil, lightly draw a line connecting the dots as shown on the pattern.

SHADOWFOLD SECRETS

Use a strong top-stitch thread so you can pull the knots tight without breaking the thread.

Start Sew Folding

7 Begin with the innermost points. Pick up just a few threads of silk within one marked point. Draw your thread through, leaving about 3 inches (7 cm) of thread.
8 At the connected point, pick up a few threads and pull the thread across.

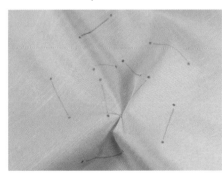

9 Trim the thread so that about 3 inches (7 cm) of thread remains.
10 Tie an overhand knot with the ends and pull the points together tightly. Make sure excess fabric doesn't get caught between the points.
11 Knot two more times to secure. Trim so that about ½ inch (1 cm) remains.
12 Continue with the remaining sets of points.

Shape the Shadowfold

13 Turn over and shape your Pentagonal Star. Flatten the twist and pleats gently with your hands.

14 For a softer, more dimensional look, iron the radiating pleats only. For a crisper star, carefully press the center.

PENTAGONAL STAR PILLOW, *continued*

Measure the Pillow's Perimeter

15 On the back of the Shadowfold, measure 2 inches (5 cm) from the outermost knot along each pleat using a square ruler. With a pencil, draw a line in both directions perpendicular to the pleat.

More Polygon Patterns

Here are a few more patterns that form stars topped with regular polygon shapes. Using the same technique, you can make a square, a hexagon, a septagon, and an octagon.

▼ Enlarge the patterns below 500% to achieve the same pleat width as the pentagon, or download using the instructions on page 24.

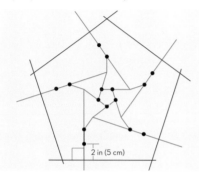

16 Continue marking the outside edge of the pentagon, connecting all lines.

Sewing the Pillow

17 Center the Shadowfold onto the remaining fabric square, right sides together, and pin.

18 Machine sew with a straight stitch along the entire line except for a 3-inch (7 cm) hole for turning right side out.

19 Trim along the sewn edge for a ½-inch (1 cm) seam allowance. Cut across each corner to make it crisper when turned right side out.

20 Turn right side out and stuff lightly with fiberfill. Evenly distribute the filling into the five corners.

21 Hand sew a blind stitch to seal the pillow's edge. ∎

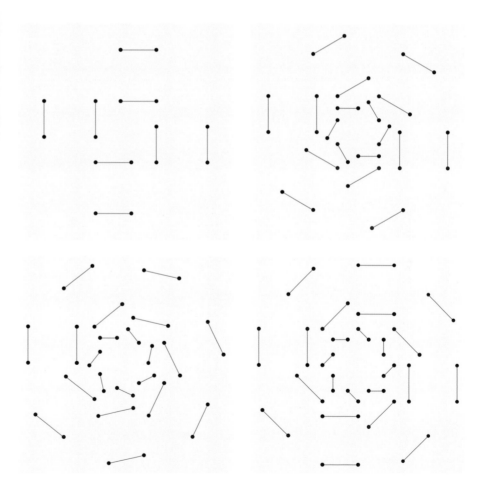

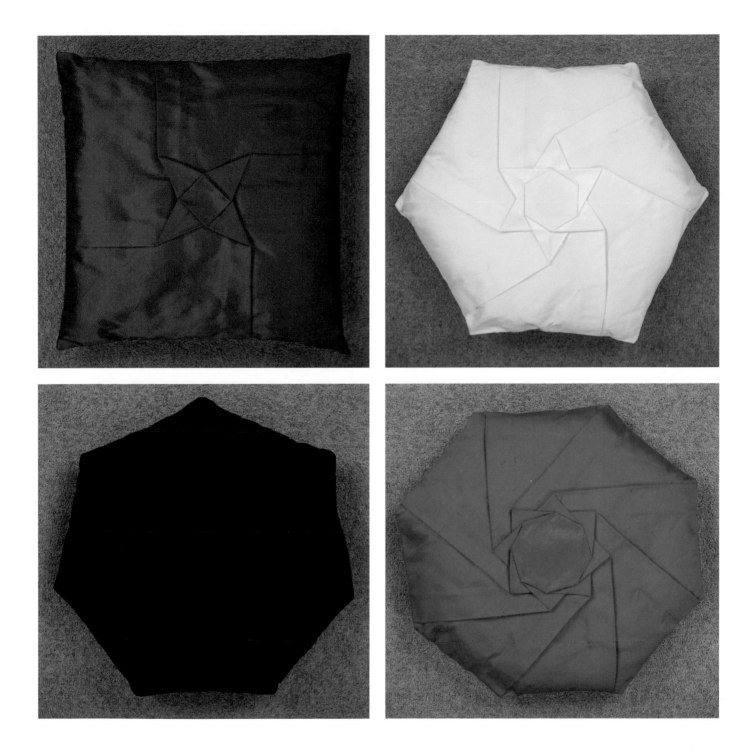

FUJIMOTO'S TWISTS

Difficulty: 🪡 | *Size:* **8½ × 8½ inches** (22 × 22 cm)
Fabric: **12 × 12 inches** (30 × 30 cm) **of silk**
Materials: **Needle, top-stitch thread, hand punch, pencil, iron, sewing machine or serger**

SHUZO FUJIMOTO IS THE FATHER OF pleated paper tessellations. This design is very easy to make and will introduce you to the four views of the classic Shadowfold.

Prepare Cloth and Transfer Pattern

1. Edge fabric with a ¼-inch (0.5 cm) hem or serge to prevent fray.
2. Enlarge the pattern on page 59 to 143% of original size, or download and print using the instructions on page 24.
3. Punch holes through the pattern at each marked circle.
4. Center pattern and tape to the fabric.
5. Mark each point using a pencil. *Double-check to be sure you've marked every point.* It's very hard to re-mark points once neighboring points are sewn together.
6. Remove the pattern and, using a pencil, lightly draw a line connecting the dots as shown on the pattern.

SHADOWFOLD SECRETS
🧵 Resist fussing with the twists and pleats on the front side until all knots are tied on the back.

Start Sew Folding

7. Begin with the center hexagon. Pick up just a few threads of silk within one marked point. Draw your thread through, leaving about 3 inches (7 cm) of thread.
8. At each connected point, pick up a few threads and pull the thread across.

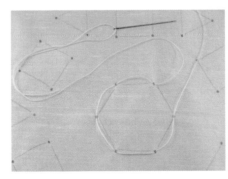

9. Trim the thread so that about 3 inches (7 cm) of thread remains.
10. Tie an overhand knot with the ends and pull the points together tightly. As each shape's points are pulled together they will form a puffy gather on the front side. Make sure excess fabric doesn't get caught between the points.

11. Knot two more times to secure. Trim so that about ½ inch (1 cm) remains.

12. Continue with the remaining sets of points until you have the pattern shown below.

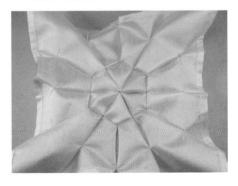

FUJIMOTO'S TWISTS, *continued*

▶▶ *Enlarge pattern to 143% of original size.*

Shape the Shadowfolds

13 Turn over and begin shaping your Fujimoto's Twists. Start with the hexagon twisted clockwise. Flatten the twist gently with your hands.

14 The direction of the pleats coming from the hexagon will inform the way each neighboring triangle or square will twist. Gently flatten each shape with your fingers until all of the twists are formed.

15 For a softer, more dimensional look, iron the radiating pleats only. For a crisper pattern, carefully press the twists and pleats. ■

THE FOUR VIEWS OF A SHADOWFOLD

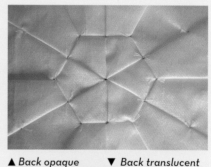

▲ *Front opaque* ▼ *Front translucent*   ▲ *Back opaque* ▼ *Back translucent*

▶ *Twists can form clockwise or counterclockwise spirals. To match the photographs in this project, twist the central hexagon clockwise.*

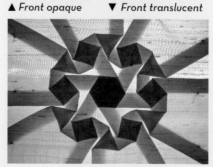

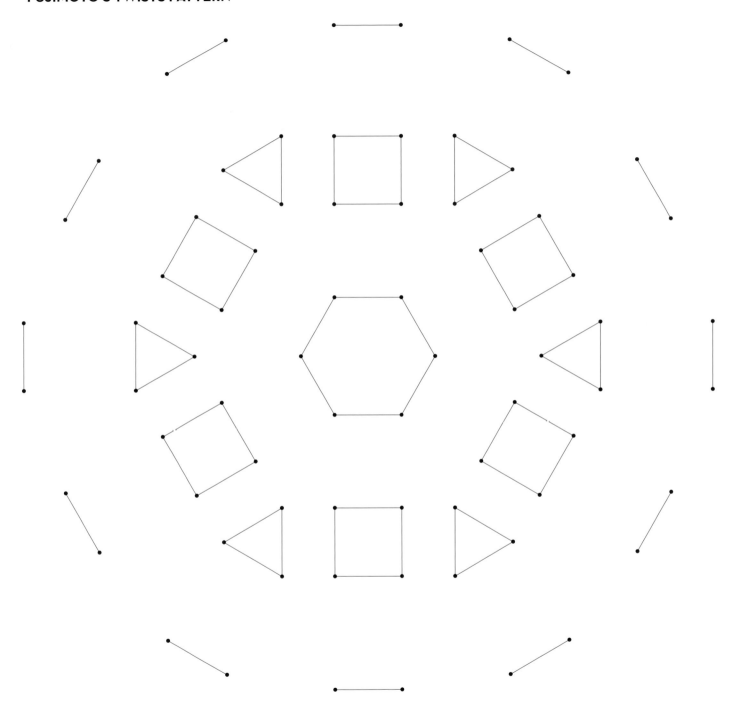

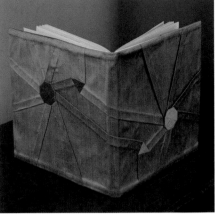

OCTAGRAM BOOK COVER

Difficulty: 🪡 | *Size:* **9 × 9 inches** (23 × 23 cm)
Fabric: **33 × 15 inches** (84 × 38 cm) **of silk or linen**
Materials: **Needle, top-stitch thread, hand punch, pencil, iron, square ruler, pins, sewing machine**

THIS COVER WILL FIT YOUR SHADOWFOLDS book, but can be easily adapted for a range of other sizes up to about 14 inches (35 cm) tall. Radiating pleats on the sides will accommodate even larger widths and pockets. The pattern may also be enlarged, if necessary.

Prepare Cloth and Transfer Pattern

1. Enlarge the pattern on page 63 to 250% of original size, or download and print using the instructions on page 24.
2. Punch holes through the pattern at each marked circle.
3. Align the pattern's reflective line, shown in pink, to the center of the fabric. Tape down to secure.

4. Mark each point using a pencil. *Double-check to be sure you've marked every point.*
5. Rotate the pattern 180°. Line up the central set of eight dots (dark blue lines) to register. Tape down to secure.
6. Mark each point for the remaining half of the fabric.
7. Remove the pattern and, using a pencil, lightly draw a line connecting the dots as shown on the pattern.

Start Sew Folding

8. Begin with the octagon twists. Pick up just a few threads of silk within one marked point. Draw your thread through, leaving about 3 inches (7 cm) of thread.

9. At each connected point, pick up a few threads and pull the thread across.
10. Trim the thread so that about 3 inches (7 cm) of thread remains.
11. Tie an overhand knot with the ends and pull the points together tightly. As each shape's points are pulled together they will form a puffy gather on the front side. Make sure excess fabric doesn't get caught between the points.
12. Knot two more times to secure. Trim so that about ½-inch (1 cm) remains.
13. Continue with the remaining sets of points until you have the pattern shown below.

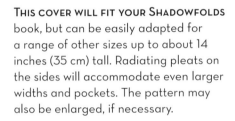

OCTAGRAM BOOK COVER, *continued*

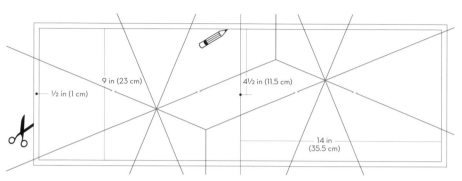

Shape the Shadowfold

14 Turn over and begin shaping the octagonal and triangular twists. The octagons twist counterclockwise and the triangles clockwise.

15 The radiating pleats should be ironed so the entire Shadowfold lies flat. Gently iron the twists flat.

Making a Book Cover for this Book

16 Using a pencil, mark the center of the piece by connecting opposite corners of the parallelogram. Then draw a vertical line through the center so that the distance *(x)* to the opposite vertical pleats is the same—about 2½ inches (6 cm).

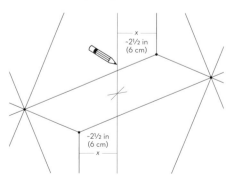

17 Measure and mark 4½ inches (11.5 cm), along the centerline, from the center towards the top edge. Repeat towards the bottom edge.

18 Using a square ruler, at each mark draw 14-inch (35.5 cm) horizontal lines, from the centerline towards the edges of the fabric, on both sides. Take care that the vertical distance between the lines remains 9 inches (23 cm). Connect the lines to form a box 28 × 9 inches (71 × 23 cm).

19 Draw an additional box ½ inch (1 cm) larger for the hem allowance and as a guide for trimming, serging, and hemming the edges.

20 For best results, serge the long, horizontal edges on the lines marked. Cut the vertical edges and fold over twice to make a ¼-inch (0.5 cm) hem.

Fit the Book Cover for this Book

21 Wrong-side out, wrap the cover around this book with the centerline along the spine. Fold the flaps inside the covers. Pin the flap edges together to fit snugly and remove cover.

22 Machine sew the flaps in place with a straight stitch, continuing along the marked line for the entire length. When turned right side out, the stitching in between the flaps will be a fold line for the serged edges.

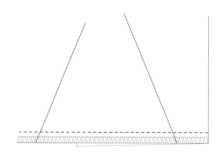

23 Turn right-side out, neaten corners, and fold edges inside along sewn seams. Iron if necessary.

24 Insert book cover into flaps. ∎

SHADOWFOLD SECRETS

Extend knots at regular intervals on radiating pleats as necessary for larger book sizes.

OCTAGRAM BOOK COVER PATTERN

▼ *Enlarge pattern to 250% of original size.*

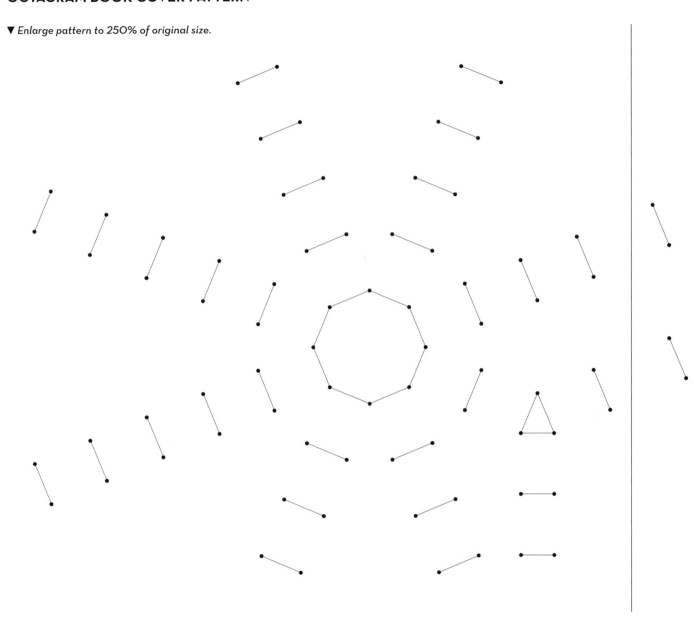

PEACE PURSE

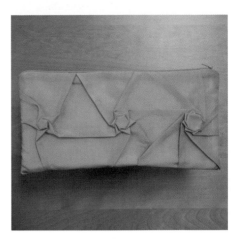

Difficulty: 🧵 | *Size:* **6 × 12 inches** (15 × 30 cm)
Fabric: **18 × 36 inches** (46 × 92 cm) **of silk or linen**
Materials: **Needle, top-stitch thread, hand punch, pencil, iron, square ruler, pins, sewing machine, 12-inch** (30 cm) **zipper**

FIVE-, SIX-, AND EIGHT-POINT STARS FLOW into each other to make a unifying pattern. This clutch's design can easily be modified to create larger sizes to piece into quilts, handbags, or to incorporate with other fashions.

Prepare Cloth and Transfer Pattern

1 Cut one 20×10 inch (51×25 cm) piece of fabric for the exterior front to be sew folded.
2 Enlarge the pattern on page 67 to 241% of original size, or download and print using the instructions on page 24.
3 Punch holes through the pattern at each marked circle.
4 Center pattern and tape to the fabric.
5 Mark each point using a pencil. *Double-check to be sure you've marked every point.*
6 Remove the pattern and, using a pencil, lightly draw a line connecting the dots as shown on the pattern.

SHADOWFOLD SECRETS

🧵 Simple patterns that tie just two dots together can be used on thicker materials, even leather.

Start Sew Folding

7 Begin with the innermost points. Pick up just a few threads of silk within one marked point. Draw your thread through, leaving about 3 inches (7 cm) of thread.
8 At its connected point, pick up a few threads and pull the thread across.

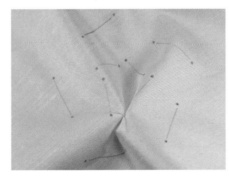

9 Trim the thread so that about 3 inches (7 cm) of thread remains.
10 Tie an overhand knot with the ends and pull the points together tightly. Make sure excess fabric doesn't get caught between the points.
11 Knot two more times to secure. Trim so that about ½ inch (1 cm) remains.
12 Continue with the remaining sets of points.

Shape the Shadowfolds

13 Turn over and shape your stars. Refer to page 53 as a guide for the six- and eight-pointed stars. Flatten the twists and pleats gently with your hands.

14 For a softer, more dimensional look, iron the radiating pleats only. For a crisper star, carefully press the center.

15 Some pleats between the stars will converge. Raise these pleats, crease, and neatly fold them down to lie in the directions shown. Iron to set firmly in place.

Assembling the Peace Purse

16 On the back of the folded front, measure a centered rectangle 13 × 7 inches (33 × 18 cm) as shown.

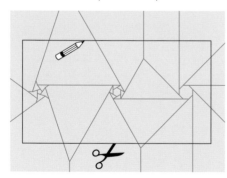

17 Cut three more 13 × 7-inch (33 × 18 cm) pieces. This includes a ½-inch (1 cm) seam allowance on all sides. Alternatively, you could use a different lining, such as a padded facing, or a linen exterior with a silk interior.

18 Assemble the folded front, right side up, the zipper face down, and one piece of the lining face down. Align edges and pin to secure. Machine-stitch along the zipper's edge, close to the teeth.

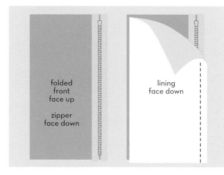

folded front face up

zipper face down

lining face down

19 Press stitched fabrics wrong sides together, away from the zipper.

20 Assemble the remaining exterior piece, right side up, the stitched fabrics with the lining face up, and the remaining lining piece face down. Align to edge of zipper and pin to secure. Machine-stitch along the zipper's edge, close to the teeth. *Note: Open the zipper about 2 inches (5 cm) for turning inside out.*

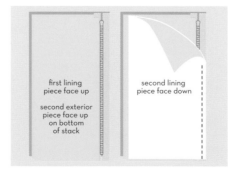

first lining piece face up

second exterior piece face up on bottom of stack

second lining piece face down

21 Press open so the exterior and interior pieces are right sides together. Align and pin to secure. Stitch along three sides, leaving the bottom of the lining open. Trim the edges and zipper, if necessary.

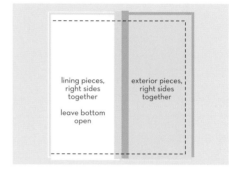

lining pieces, right sides together

exterior pieces, right sides together

leave bottom open

22 Unzip the zipper all the way and turn the lining right sides out, folded over the exterior. Turn under the bottom edge of the lining about ¼-inch (0.5 cm) and pin to secure. Stitch across, making sure not to catch the exterior pieces inside.

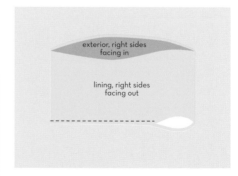

exterior, right sides facing in

lining, right sides facing out

23 Turn right side out and tuck the lining inside. ∎

PEACE PURSE PATTERN

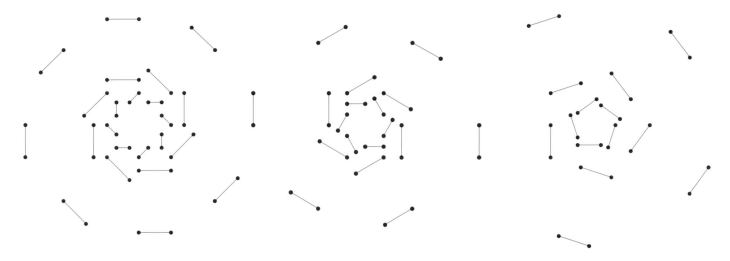

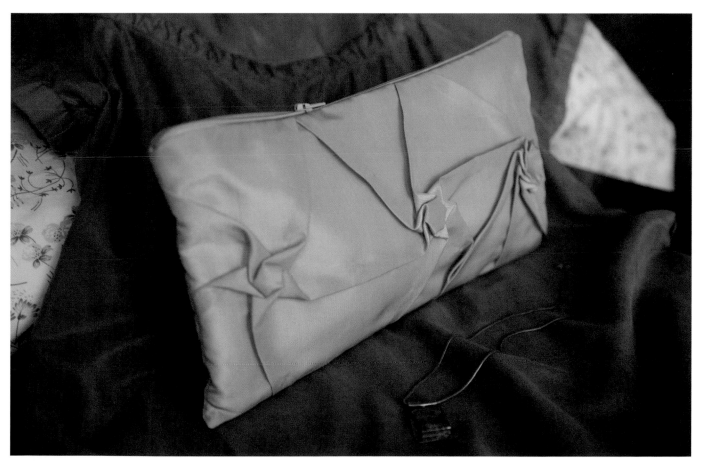

PINWHEEL PATH

Difficulty: 🔔🔔 | *Size:* **11 × 18 inches** (28 × 46 cm)
Fabric: **22 × 36 inches** (56 × 92 cm) **of silk**
Materials: **Needle, top-stitch thread, hand punch, pencil, iron, sewing machine or serger**

CREATE A STUNNING AND TIMELESS DESIGN that expands upon Fujimoto's Twists. This Shadowfold looks best when framed between two sheets of acrylic and hung in a window.

Prepare Cloth and Transfer Pattern

1 Edge fabric with a ¼-inch (0.5 cm) hem or serge to prevent fray.
2 Enlarge the pattern on page 71 to 250% of original size, or download and print using the instructions on page 24.
3 Punch holes through the pattern at each marked circle.
4 Align the pattern's reflective line, shown in pink, to the center of the fabric. Tape down to secure.

5 Mark each point using a pencil. *Double-check to be sure you've marked every point.*
6 Rotate the pattern 180°. Line up the central column of dark blue shapes to register. Tape down to secure.
7 Mark each point for the remaining half of the fabric.
8 Remove the pattern and, using a pencil, lightly draw a line connecting the dots as shown on the pattern.

Start Sew Folding

9 Begin with the innermost points. Pick up just a few threads of silk within one marked point. Draw your thread through, leaving about 3 inches (7 cm) of thread.

10 At each connected point, pick up a few threads and pull the thread across.
11 Trim the thread so that about 3 inches (7 cm) of thread remains.
12 Tie an overhand knot with the ends and pull the points together tightly. As each shape's points are pulled together they will form a puffy gather on the front side. Make sure excess fabric doesn't get caught between the points.
13 Knot two more times to secure. Trim so that about ½ inch (1 cm) remains.
14 Continue with the remaining sets of points until you have the pattern shown below.

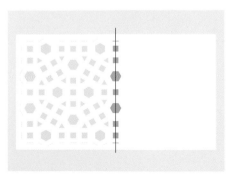

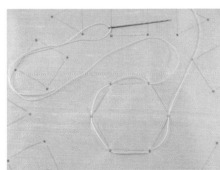

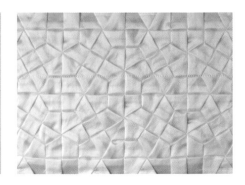

PINWHEEL PATH, *continued*

▶▶ *Enlarge pattern to 250% of original size.*

Shape the Shadowfolds

15 Turn over and begin shaping your Pinwheel Path. Start with the hexagon twisted clockwise. Flatten the twist gently with your hands.

16 The direction of the pleats coming from the hexagon will inform the way each neighboring triangle or square will twist. Gently flatten each shape with your fingers until all of the twists are formed.

17 For a softer, more dimensional look, iron the edge pleats only. For a crisper pattern, carefully press all of the twists and pleats. ■

▶ *Twists can form clockwise or counterclockwise spirals. To match the photographs in this project, twist the central square counterclockwise.*

▶*All pleats will lie flat if twists spiral in the correct direction. Reverse any twists to fix connecting pleats that still stand up.*

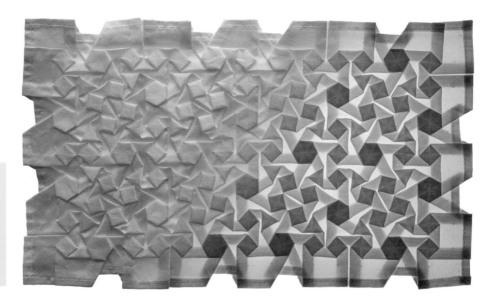

SHADOWFOLD SECRETS

 This Shadowfold can easily be made as a square, too, by only using the half-pattern shown. Rotate it 180° to repeat the edge knots on the left to mark the right-hand side.

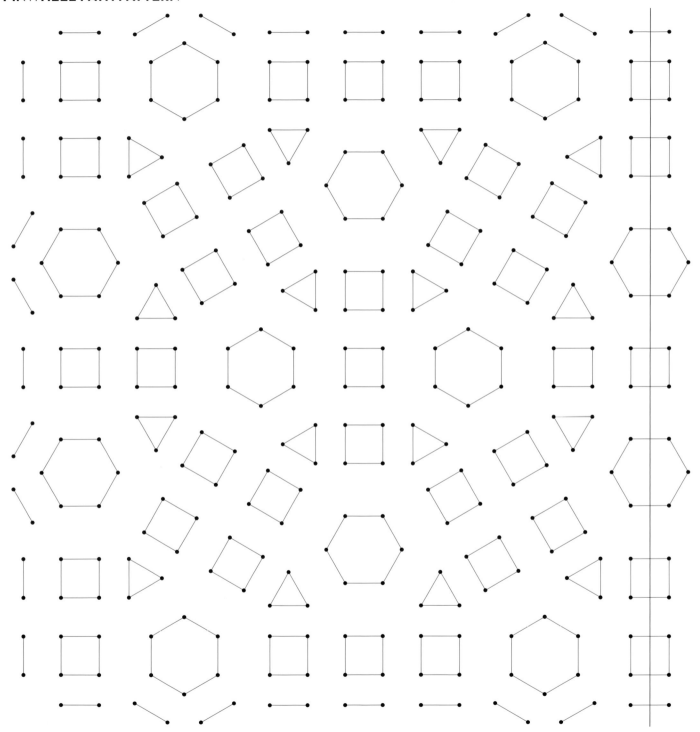

STAR-FLOWER PILLBOX HAT

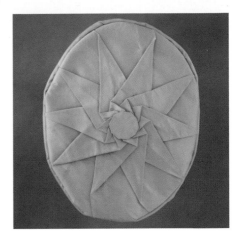

Difficulty: 🎀🎀 | *Size:* **7³⁄4 × 6¹⁄2 × 3 inches** (19.5 × 16.5 × 7 cm)
Fabric: **24 × 20 inches** (61 × 51 cm) **of silk or linen, padded facing**
Materials: **Needle, top-stitch thread, hand punch, pencil, iron, pins, sewing machine, tape measure**

THIS NOSTALGIC HAT FEATURES A COMPLEX decagram star, but the hat's construction is simple. This style can be worn by women or men. For men, choose a dark-colored linen.

Prepare Cloth and Transfer Pattern

1 Enlarge the pattern on page 75 to 200% of original size, or download and print using the instructions on page 24.
2 Punch holes through the dot pattern at each marked circle.
3 Cut one 15×15 inch (38×38 cm) silk square; reserve the rest for the band.
4 Center pattern and tape to the fabric.
5 Mark each point using a pencil. *Double-check to be sure you've marked every point.*
6 Remove the pattern and, using a pencil, lightly draw a line connecting the dots as shown on the pattern.
7 Begin with the center decagon. Pick up just a few threads of silk within one marked point. Draw your thread through, leaving about 3 inches (7 cm) of thread.
8 At each connected point, pick up a few threads and pull the thread across.

9 Trim the thread so that about 3 inches (7 cm) of thread remains.
10 Tie an overhand knot with the ends and pull the points together tightly. As each shape's points are pulled together they will form a puffy gather on the front side. Make sure excess fabric doesn't get caught between the points.
11 Knot two more times to secure. Trim so that about ¹⁄2 inch (1 cm) remains.
12 To make it easier to sew the four-sided shapes around the decagon, begin with the narrow end. Pick up the *innermost* point and work clockwise to connect the dots. After knotting the shape, continue clockwise to the next shape's narrow end.

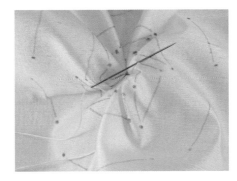

13 Continue with the remaining sets of points until you have the pattern shown below.

Shape the Shadowfold

14 Shape the decagon twist by rotating it clockwise. Shape the inner petals counterclockwise as shown. Press flat with the tip of your iron.

15 On the back, make a crease with your thumbnail, connecting all of the outer knots in a straight line. Press flat.

16 On the front, the large outer petals will lie counterclockwise atop one another, while the radiating pleats will lie in a clockwise pattern. Press flat.

Making a Pillbox Hat from the Shadowfold

17 Photocopy the oval pattern on page 116 or download and print using the instructions on page 24. Cut out.

18 Center and tape the oval on the right side of the Shadowfold. Insert pins from the right side at the four points

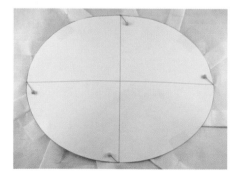

along the edge of the oval. The pin points should be straight down and will be used for alignment in Step 21.

19 Cut out a 9×10 inch (23×26 cm) piece of the padded facing.

20 Remove the paper oval from the Shadowfold and tape it to the facing right side up. Trace the oval and mark the four edge points.

21 Remove the paper oval from the facing. Place facing atop the Shadowfold, wrong sides together, by inserting the pin points so they align with the marks along the edges. Pin the facing to the Shadowfold outside the perimeter of the oval and remove the marking pins.

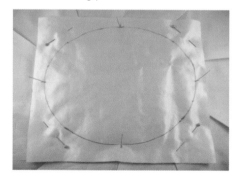

22 Using a ½-inch (1 cm) seam allowance *outside* the marked line, sew the Shadowfold and facing together. Trim close to the seam.

23 Cut out 4×23 inch (10×58.5 cm) pieces of the padded facing and silk.

24 Pin right sides together and sew along the long edge using a ½-inch (1 cm) seam allowance.

25 Turn right side out and press the seam inside. Pin the short edges

together with the silk on the inside. Sew along the short edges using a ½-inch (1 cm) seam allowance.

26 Carefully pin the band's raw edges to the top along the perimeter, right sides together.

27 Machine sew along the marked line. Work very slowly to avoid puckering the edges. Turn right side out. ■

STAR-FLOWER PILLBOX HAT PATTERN

▼ *Enlarge pattern to 200% of original size.*

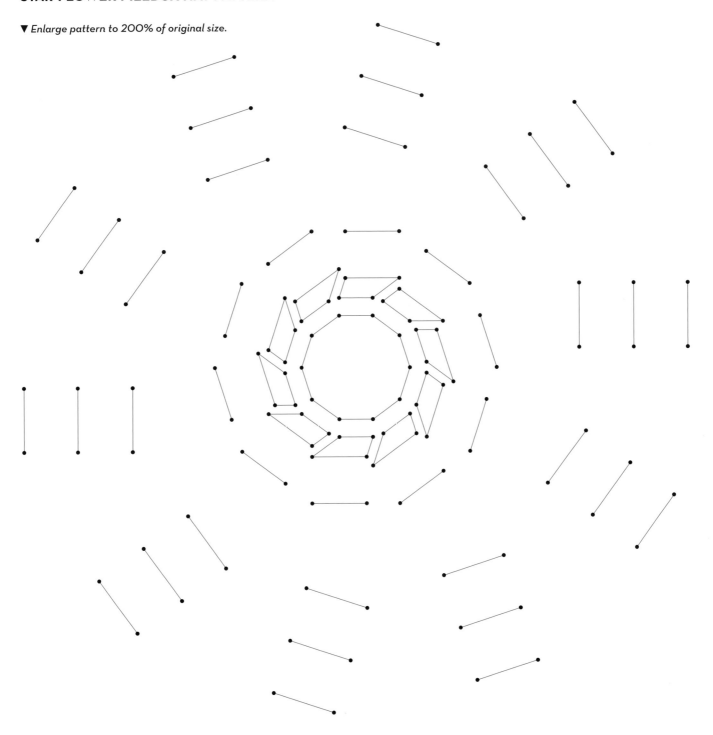

TWIST NECKTIE

Difficulty: 🎀🎀 | *Size:* **4 × 56 inches** (10 × 142 cm)
Fabric: **36 × 36 inches** (91 × 91 cm) **of silk, recycled necktie**
Materials: **Needle, top-stitch thread, hand punch, pencil, iron, pins, sewing machine, safety pin**

MAKE AN ELEGANT NECKTIE USING JUST a few simple square twists. This project, like the Peace Purse, illustrates the ease of taking a sew folded piece and turning it into a fashion accessory.

Prepare Cloth and Transfer Pattern

1 Enlarge the pattern on page 117 to 450% of original size, or download and print using the instructions on page 24.

2 Cut out the pattern pieces. Only cut to the outer line of the wide end's piece. You will trim to the inner line *after* making the twists and pleats.

3 Punch holes through the dot pattern at each marked circle.

4 Pin the pattern pieces to the silk, aligning the arrows with the grain. Cut out the pieces of silk.

5 Mark each point using a pencil. *Double-check to be sure you've marked every point.*

6 Remove the pattern and, using a pencil, lightly draw a line connecting the dots as shown on the pattern.

7 Begin with the center square. Pick up just a few threads of silk within one marked point. Draw your thread

through, leaving about 3 inches (7 cm) of thread.

8 At each connected point, pick up a few threads and pull the thread across.

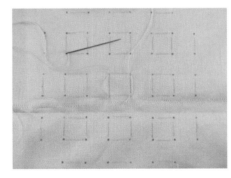

9 Trim the thread so that about 3 inches (7 cm) of thread remains.

10 Tie an overhand knot with the ends and pull the points together tightly. As each shape's points are pulled together they will form a puffy gather on the front side. Make sure excess fabric doesn't get caught between the points.

SHADOWFOLD SECRETS
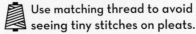 Use matching thread to avoid seeing tiny stitches on pleats.

11 Knot two more times to secure. Trim so that about ½-inch (1 cm) remains.

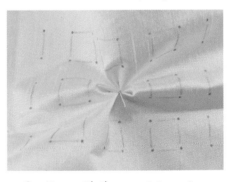

12 Continue with the remaining sets of points until you have the pattern shown below.

TWIST NECKTIE, *continued*

Shape the Shadowfold

13 Turn over and begin shaping the square twists. The central square twist is counterclockwise in the photos.

14 The radiating pleats should be ironed very carefully, extending evenly to the edges so the entire Shadowfold lies flat. For a softer, more dimensional look, do not iron the twists.

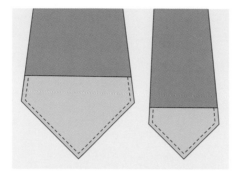
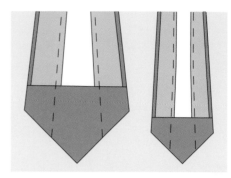

Making a Necktie from the Shadowfold

15 Trim the pattern for the wide end to the inner line. Pin the pattern back onto the pressed Shadowfold piece and trim the silk. Remove the pattern.

16 Pin the *back* of the middle piece to the fronts of the wide and narrow ends. Offset the short edges of the ends about ½ inch (1 cm) as shown.

17 Using a ½-inch (1 cm) seam allowance, sew the wide and narrow ends to the middle piece.

18 Press the seams flat and trim the small triangles on the edges.

19 Pin the wide tip to the *front* of the wide end, and the narrow tip to the *front* of the narrow end.

20 Using a ½-inch (1 cm) seam allowance, sew the tips to the end pieces together at the edges.

21 Turn out the tips, using a pin to nudge out the corners, if necessary.

22 Fold over the long sides ½ inch (1 cm) and iron to make an even edge with the tips.

23 Take apart a recycled necktie to free the woven interfacing inside.

24 Insert the wide end of the interfacing all of the way inside the wide tip of the tie. If necessary, trim the narrow end to fit inside the narrow tip.

25 Narrow the tie by folding in thirds. Carefully center the square twists.

The wide end should be about 4 inches (10 cm) across the corners and the narrow end about 1½ inches (4 cm). When satisfied with the shape, iron flat.

26 Fold the overlapping flap under so the edge is centered along the entire length of the back. Iron flat and pin in place.

27 To make the keeper, sew the long edges together. Trim the seam allowance to a ¼ inch (0.5 cm). Turn seam inside using a safety pin. Sew the short edges together but do not trim. Press the ends of the loop so that the seam is in the middle, but keep its edges together.

28 Position the keeper about 9 inches (23 cm) from the wide end and insert its seam underneath the center fold. Hand sew the seam to the top flap.

29 Using a slipstitch, hand sew the top and bottom flaps along the entire length of the tie.

30 Secure the corners of the keeper down on the back. ■

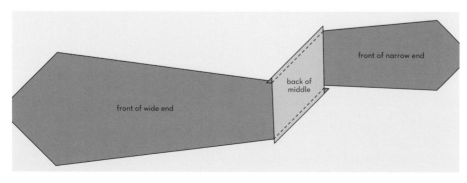

front of wide end

back of middle

front of narrow end

DODECAGON WHIRL SPOOLS

Difficulty: 🔔🔔 | *Size:* **15 × 15 inches** (38 × 38 cm)
Fabric: **36 × 36 inches** (91 × 91 cm) **of silk**
Materials: **Needle, top-stitch thread, hand punch, pencil, iron, ruler, sewing machine, serger (optional)**

THIS SHADOWFOLD PROJECT REINFORCES that something that looks complex isn't always hard to make. Repeating Dodecagon Whirl Spools is easy. A hemmed version of this pattern, made into a long valance, is shown on page 18.

Prepare Cloth and Transfer Pattern

1 Enlarge the pattern on page 83 to 278% of original size, or download and print using the instructions on page 24.
2 Punch holes through the pattern at each marked circle.
3 This pattern will rotate twice to complete the finished design. Align the intersection of the pattern's reflective lines, shown in pink, to the center of the fabric. Tape down to secure.

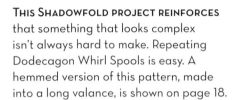

4 Mark each point using a pencil. *Double-check to be sure you've marked every point.*
5 Rotate the pattern 120° by lining up one of the pink lines on top of the other. Be sure the central marks (and some side marks in between the dodecagons) show through to register. Tape down to secure.
6 Mark each point not previously marked. Repeat Step 5 to complete.
7 Remove the pattern and, using a pencil, lightly draw a line connecting the dots as shown on the pattern.

Decide Whether to Hem or Serge Edge

The photos here show a simple satin stitch edge, trimmed. This is done *after* sew folding and ironing. To finish in this way, proceed to Step 13. If you want an edge similar to the valance shown on page 18, then you must finish the edge *before* sew folding begins. Follow the next few steps first.

Finishing the Edge Beforehand

10 Connect the six outermost dots (the ones not connected to any others) to make a hexagon.

11 Cut out the hexagon ¼ inch (0.5 cm) *outside* of the line.
12 Edge fabric with a ¼-inch (0.5 cm) hem or serge at the marked line to prevent fray.

Start Sew Folding

13 Begin with the dodecagon twists. Pick up just a few threads of silk within one marked point. Draw your thread through, leaving about 3 inches (7 cm) of thread.
14 At each connected point, pick up a few threads and pull the thread across.
15 Trim the thread so that about 3 inches (7 cm) of thread remains.
16 Tie an overhand knot with the ends and pull the points together tightly.

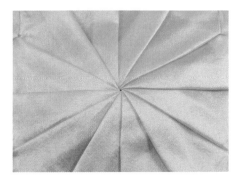

DODECAGON WHIRL SPOOLS, *continued*

As each shape's points are pulled together they will form a puffy gather on the front side. Make sure excess fabric doesn't get caught between the points.

17 Knot two more times to secure. Trim so that about ½-inch (1 cm) remains.

18 Continue with the remaining sets of points until you have the pattern shown below.

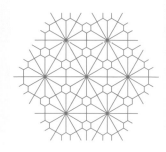

Shape the Shadowfold

19 Turn over and begin shaping the dodecagon twists, flattening them in a clockwise direction. Squares will twist counterclockwise, however each triangle's direction will alternate, depending on whether the pleats

come from its adjacent square, or the dodecagon.

20 The edge pleats should be ironed so the entire Shadowfold lies flat. Gently iron the twists flat.

Finishing the Edge Afterwards

21 Re-iron the edge pleats crisp from the back.

22 On the back, locate the six outer dots that were not sew folded into shapes. Draw a line connecting these into a hexagon along the perimeter.

23 Serge the entire perimeter. Alternatively, sew a tight, wide satin stitch, and trim close to the outer edge to finish. ∎

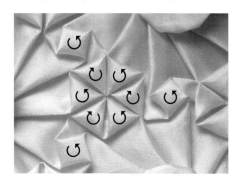

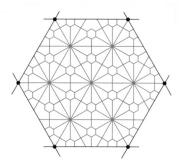

SHADOWFOLD SECRETS

Practice finishing the edges first on a scrap with some pleats ironed in. Be careful not to snag any pleats under the presser foot or the feed dogs.

DODECAGON WHIRL SPOOLS PATTERN

▼ *Enlarge pattern to 278% of original size.*

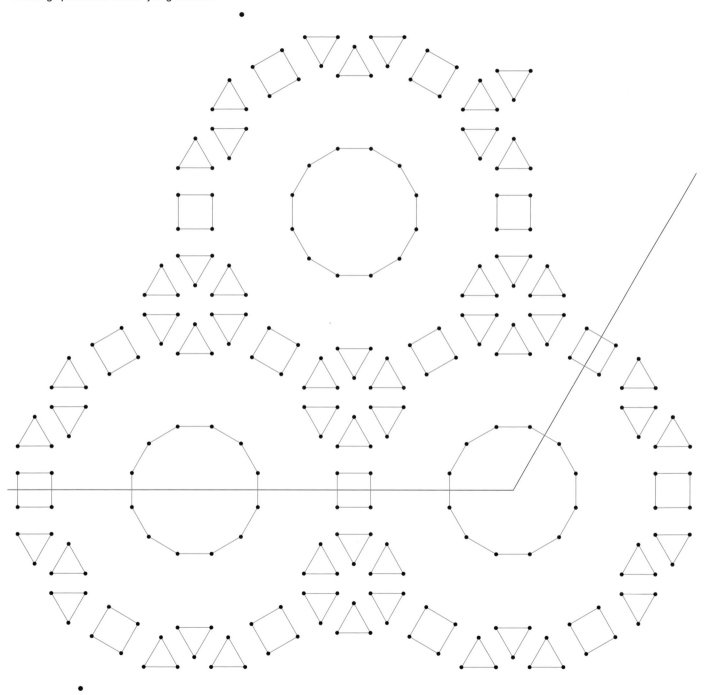

OCTAGON BEDSPREAD

Difficulty: 🔺🔺 | *Size:* **Variable, depending on starting fabric**
Fabric: **Plain-woven bedspread from a department store**
Materials: **Needle, top-stitch thread, hand punch, pencil, iron, yard** (meter) **stick, pins, roll of kraft paper**

THIS PROJECT INTRODUCES A TECHNIQUE to make very large Shadowfolds. By purchasing a factory-made bedspread, you eliminate the need to find very wide cloth as well as finish its long edges. Choose a plain texture, or opt for a large-scale, *non-geometric*, satin pattern as show in the photos. This will make a subtle contrast to the twists and pleats.

Prepare Pattern by Using a Grid
Patterns that are too large to print and tile together can be marked onto large paper using a grid. Flatten two 40-inch (100 cm) sections of at least a 20-inch (50 cm) wide roll of kraft paper. *Make sure the edges are square.* Or use two large sheets that are at least 40 × 20 inches (100 × 50 cm).

1 Tape together the two sheets to make a 40 × 40-inch (100 × 100 cm) surface.
2 Using a long ruler, draw a ½-inch (1 cm) margin from the edges.
3 Reference the pattern on page 87 and draw each pink line shown, beginning with the lower-left corner of the margin. Number each line along the *x* and *y* axes.
4 Mark a dot at each coordinate shown on the pattern. *Double-check to be sure you've marked every point correctly.* Connect the dots as shown.
5 Punch holes through the pattern at each marked circle.
6 Find the center of your bedspread by folding into quarters. Iron the layers and creases neatly.

7 Unfold, right side down, onto a large hard surface, such as a clean kitchen floor. Only the upper-right quarter needs to be perfectly flat at this time. However, if the edges hang off of a table, their weight might distort the fabric.
8 Align the pattern's reflective lines, shown in heavier pink, along the creased lines of the fabric. Make sure the (O,O) point is at the center of the fabric, and the dots align along each creased axis. You might have to adjust the fabric underneath to "square it" with the pattern. Tape down to secure.
9 Mark each point using a pencil. *Double-check to be sure you've marked every point.*

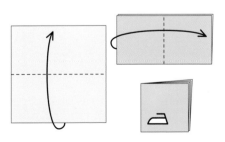

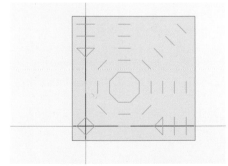

40 in (100 cm)
40 in (100 cm)

OCTAGON BEDSPREAD, *continued*

10 Remove the pattern and, using a pencil, lightly draw a line connecting the dots as shown on the pattern.

11 Rotate the pattern 90°. Align the set of dots along the axis with the previously-marked dots. Repeat Steps 8–11 until the four sections are completely marked.

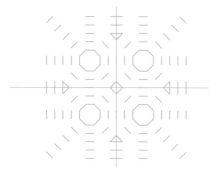

Start Sew Folding

12 Begin with the octagon twists. Pick up about 1/16 inch (2 mm) of fabric over one marked point. Draw your thread through, leaving about 3 inches (7 cm) of thread.

13 At each connected point, pick up about 1/16 inch (2 mm) of fabric and pull the thread across.

14 Trim the thread so that about 3 inches (7 cm) of thread remains.

15 Tie an overhand knot with the ends and pull the points together tightly. As each shape's points are pulled together they will form a puffy gather on the front side. Make sure excess fabric doesn't get caught between the points.

16 Knot three more times to secure. Trim so that about 1 inch (2 cm) remains.

17 Continue with the remaining sets of points until you have the pattern shown below.

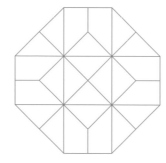

Shape the Shadowfold

18 For this project to lie flat, opposite-corner octagons will twist counter-clockwise while adjacent ones will twist clockwise. Begin by shaping any octagonal twist and follow its radiating pleat towards the next and twist in the opposite way until those pleats lie flat. Continue with the remaining octagons.

19 The central square does not twist, but instead will squash flat. Follow the converging pleats from the octagons toward the center, and push the

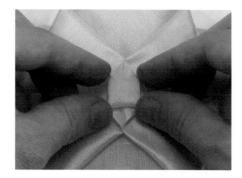

fabric together to form the raised point of a triangle. Insert your fingers in the pockets on either side of the triangle. Spread the sides, and nudge the raised point so it flattens into the center of a square.

20 The remaining pleats between adjacent octagons will converge in one of two ways:

- *Pleats that lie toward the center:* Follow the converging pleats from the octagons and push the fabric together along a sloping side, then simply lay the pleat flat to the right.
- *Pleats that lie away from the center:* Follow the converging pleats from the octagons to end in a point. Then push the fabric to the right to flatten.

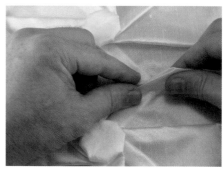

21 Iron all pleats and twists using steam to set firmly. ∎

SHADOWFOLD SECRETS

This pattern could be easily scaled down to make a design for a tablecloth or a child's bedspread. Center it on a round, oval, square, or rectangular shape.

OCTAGON BEDSPREAD PATTERN

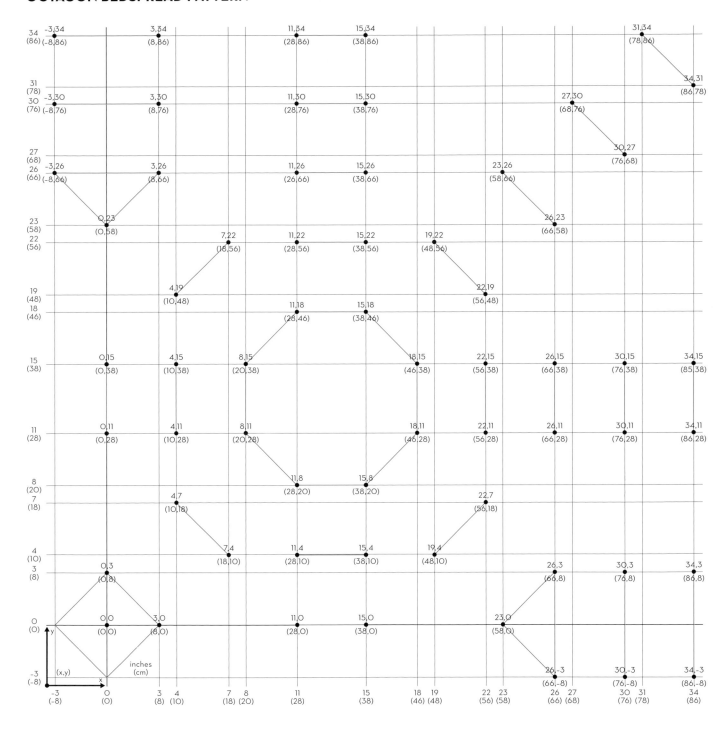

PINWHEEL PATH LAMP

Difficulty: 🪡🪡 | *Size:* **7 × 18 inches** (18 × 46 cm)
Fabric: **28 × 36 inches** (71 × 91 cm) **of silk**
Materials: **Needle, top-stitch thread, hand punch, pencil, iron, ruler, pins, sewing machine, lamp hoops, hanging lamp socket, glue**

A GREAT WAY TO ENJOY A SHADOWFOLD is to see its opaque and translucent patterns with the flip of a switch. This project was designed to use off-the-shelf hardware available at some lamp parts stores. It's the first Shadowfold to be made into a 360° continuous pattern.

Prepare Cloth and Transfer Pattern

1 Enlarge the patterns on pages 118–119 to 286% of original size, or download and print using the instructions on page 24. The pattern dimensions must be exact so the final tube's diameter will be 7 inches (18 cm).

2 Tape together both pattern pieces along the dotted lines, overlapping the shapes. The width should be 33½ inches (85 cm) between the pink lines.

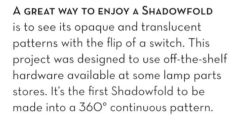

3 Punch holes through the pattern at each marked circle.

4 Center the pattern onto the fabric and tape down to secure.

5 Mark each point using a pencil, including the four points on the pink lines. *Double-check to be sure you've marked every point.*

6 Remove the pattern and, using a pencil, lightly draw a line connecting the dots as shown on the pattern. Use a ruler to connect the dots for the pink lines and extend the lines past the dots to the edges of the fabric.

Sew the Fabric into a Tube

7 Pin the fabric, right sides together, so the end lines overlap one another perfectly. Machine sew a seam along

the line. Trim to a ¼ inch (0.5 cm) and press flat.

Start Sew Folding

8 Begin with the hexagon twists. Pick up just a few threads of silk within one marked point. Draw your thread through, leaving about 3 inches (7 cm) of thread.

9 At each connected point, pick up a few threads and pull the thread across.

10 Trim the thread so that about 3 inches (7 cm) of thread remains.

11 Tie an overhand knot with the ends and pull the points together tightly. As each shape's points are pulled together they will form a puffy gather on the inside of the tube. Make sure excess fabric doesn't get caught between the points.

12 Knot two more times to secure. Trim so that about ½-inch (1 cm) remains.

13 Continue with the remaining sets of points until you have the pattern shown on the next page. Where two shapes connect across the seam, neatly tuck the seam allowance to avoid any buckling.

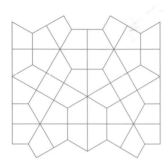

Shape the Shadowfold

14 Turn the tube right side out and begin with any hexagonal twist. It doesn't matter which way you twist, clockwise or counterclockwise, but the radiating pleats will inform each and every other shape's direction. Gently flatten each shape with your fingers until all of the twists are formed.

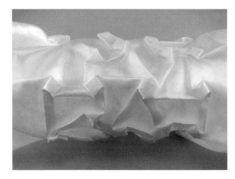

15 Using a sleeve board, iron the pleats along the seam so they lie flat neatly. Continue rotating the tube and slowly iron the remaining pleats. Gently iron the twists flat.

Assembling the Pinwheel Path Lamp

This lamp was designed to avoid any frame that might show through the Shadowfold, thus interrupting the geometric patterns. Only two 7-inch (18 cm) hoops hold it together. The top hoop, known as a "spider," has a center ring to hang a corded socket. The bottom hoop is just a plain ring, whose weight alone will pull the Shadowfold down into a cylinder.

The hardware can be found at some lamp parts stores; the corded socket at any IKEA (see Resources on page 124).

16 Turn the tube inside out and gently flatten with the seam along one edge. Do not iron.

17 Trim the top and bottom straight across about 3 inches (7 cm) from the first and last rows of twists. If necessary, use a square ruler to mark the cuts perpendicular to the seam.

18 Roll a ¼-inch (0.5 cm) hem on both ends, ironing using a sleeve board. Pin to secure.

19 Machine sew the hems. Turn the tube right side out, and if necessary, re-iron any pleats and twists.

20 Glue the bottom hem to the metal hoop. If your hoop has a flange, glue it to the inside of the flange. If your hoop is just a ring, glue it to the outside of the ring. Hold the tube upright until the glue sets, without raising the lamp off your work surface.

21 Similarly, glue the top hem to the metal hoop. Hold the tube upright until the glue sets, without raising the lamp off your work surface.

22 Choose a bulb not more than 60 watts. Incandescent tubular bulbs come in lengths as long as 10 inches (25 cm), are dimmable, and will distribute the light evenly throughout the lamp.

23 Center the bulb and socket within the lamp and fix its position in the center hole of the top hoop.

24 Hang your Pinwheel Path Lamp and enjoy both views with the flick of a switch. ∎

SHADOWFOLD SECRETS

This lampshade design will also work on a simple pole-style lamp. The bulb, however, may be more difficult to center within the Shadowfold. Sourcing a top "spider" ring that mounts onto the bulb base will be more challenging.

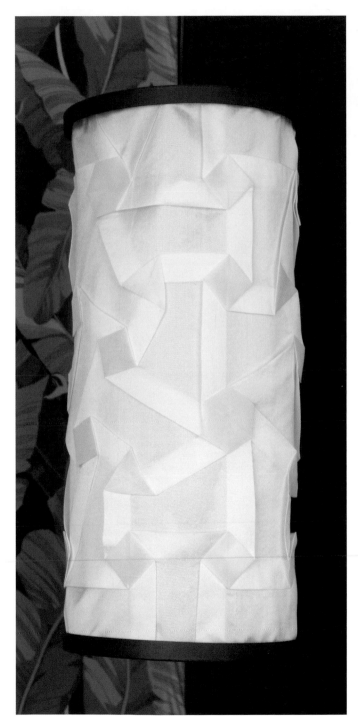

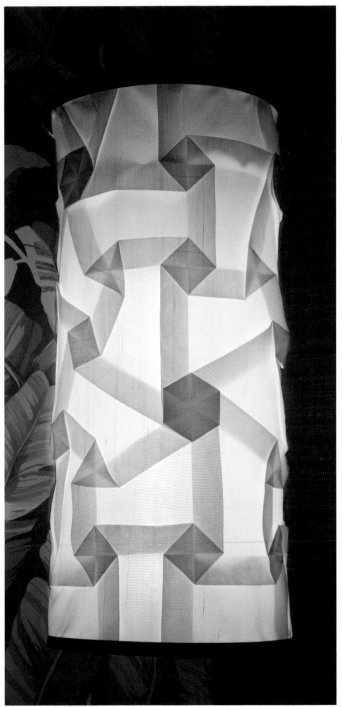

STAR OF DAVID ROSETTE

Difficulty: 🔔🔔 | *Size:* **20 × 20 inches** (51 × 51 cm)
Fabric: **30 × 30 inches** (76 × 76 cm) **of silk**
Materials: **Needle, top-stitch thread, hand punch, pencil, iron, sewing machine, serger (optional)**

SHADOWFOLD ROSETTES ARE DESIGNED from a geometry that can expand outward rapidly to repeat the motif. There is a nice contrast between the detailed center and the widening pleats and unfolded spaces. This simple rosette introduces new folding techniques you will also use for the next two projects.

Prepare Cloth and Transfer Pattern

1 Enlarge the pattern on page 95 to 333% of original size, or download and print using the instructions on page 24.
2 Punch holes through the pattern at each marked circle.
3 Center pattern and tape to the fabric.
4 Mark each point using a pencil. *Double-check to be sure you've marked every point.*
5 Remove the pattern and, using a pencil, lightly draw a line connecting the dots as shown on the pattern.
6 Hem or serge the edges about 2-3 inches (5-7 cm) from the outermost dots on the pattern.

Start Sew Folding

7 Begin with the central hexagon twist. Pick up just a few threads of silk within one marked point. Draw your thread through, leaving about 3 inches (7 cm) of thread.
8 At each connected point, pick up a few threads and pull the thread across.
9 Trim the thread so that about 3 inches (7 cm) of thread remains.
10 Tie an overhand knot with the ends and pull the points together tightly. As each shape's points are pulled together they will form a puffy gather on the front side. Make sure excess fabric doesn't get caught between the points.
11 Knot two more times to secure. Trim so that about ½-inch (1 cm) remains.
12 Continue with the remaining sets of points until you have the pattern shown at right.

Shape the Shadowfold

13 Turn over and begin shaping the center hexagon twist, flattening it in a clockwise direction.

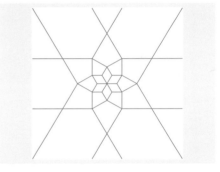

14 The ring of pleats surrounding the center hexagon forms the first Star of David. Lift the three intersecting pleats with your thumbs and forefingers and crease to form a raised point.

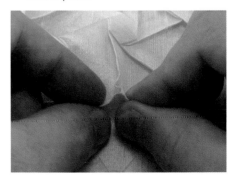

15 Lay the pleats flat towards the center while simultaneously tucking the pleat from the hexagon underneath the other two.

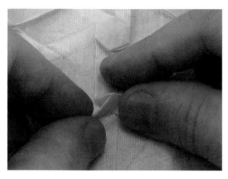

16 Repeat Steps 14-15 for the remaining five points along the first ring.

17 The second ring of pleats is a bit trickier to fold. Lift the four intersecting pleats with your thumbs and forefingers and crease to form a raised point.

18 Lay the pleats flat towards the center while simultaneously tucking the pleats from the first ring underneath the second ring. Form two small triangles that are completely covered by the top layer of the second ring.

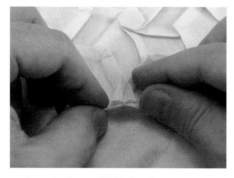

19 Repeat Steps 17-18 for the remaining five points along the second ring.

20 The third ring of pleats folds flat in the same method as the second ring. The hidden triangles are easier to fold neatly since the pleats are wider.

21 The final ring of pleats also folds flat similarly, except the four intersecting pleats don't form a raised point. Instead they make a trapezoid shape. The triangles underneath extend past the top edge, forming neat points.

22 Extend the top layer of pleats out to the edges of the fabric.

23 Iron the pleats gently, taking care to keep the underlying triangles neat and evenly extended. ∎

SHADOWFOLD SECRETS
 The Star of David Rosette is a pattern that is easy to make into a pillow or pillow sham, although you won't see the hidden, translucent design. For a pillow sham, extend the fabric along the pleats that radiate horizontally and adjust the dimensions for your pillow's size.

STAR OF DAVID ROSETTE PATTERN

▼ *Enlarge pattern to 333% of original size.*

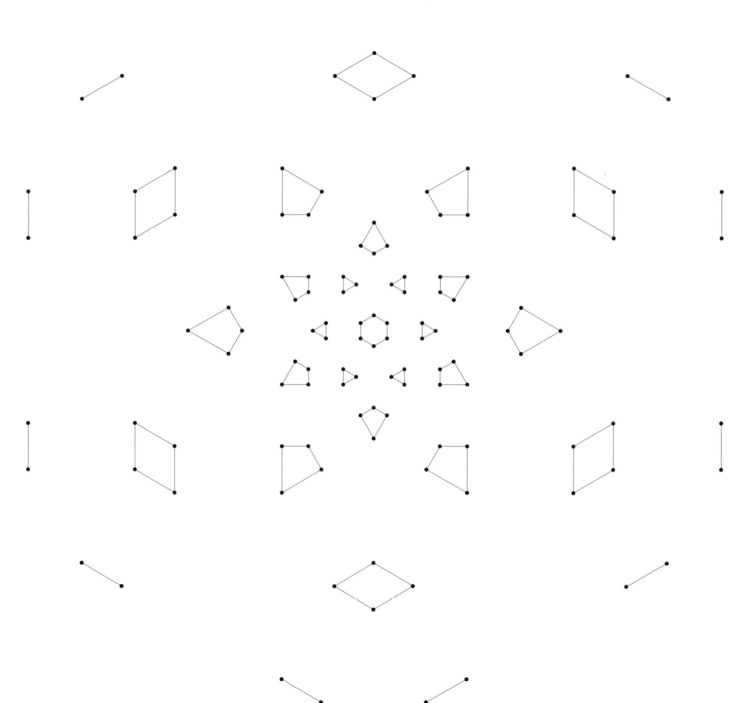

RADIATING ROSETTE

Difficulty: 🔔🔔 | *Size:* **20 × 20 inches** (51 × 51 cm)
Fabric: **30 × 30 inches** (76 × 76 cm) **of silk**
Materials: **Needle, top-stitch thread, hand punch, pencil, iron, sewing machine, serger (optional)**

ONE OF THE MOST EXTRAORDINARY Shadowfold designs is the Radiating Rosette. Reminiscent of many botanic forms, the rosette design is used extensively in architecture. This 12-sided rosette is similar to one crafted from marble on the floor of the Duomo in Florence. The backlit design is also striking, as shown on page 2. *Rosette Flag* is a much larger example, shown in the Gallery on page 47.

Prepare Cloth and Transfer Pattern

1 Enlarge the pattern on page 99 to 200% of original size, or download and print using the instructions on page 24.
2 Punch holes through the pattern at each marked circle.

3 Align the pattern's reflective lines, shown in pink, so their intersection is in the center of the fabric. Tape down to secure.
4 Mark each point using a pencil. *Double-check to be sure you've marked every point.*
5 Rotate the pattern 90°. Line up the shapes on the pink line. Tape down to secure.
6 Mark each point for the remaining quadrants of the fabric.
7 Remove the pattern and, using a pencil, lightly draw a line connecting the dots as shown on the pattern.
8 Hem or serge the edges about 2 inches (5 cm) from the outermost dots on the pattern.

Start Sew Folding

9 Begin with the dodecagon twist. Pick up just a few threads of silk within one marked point. Draw your thread through, leaving about 3 inches (7 cm) of thread.
10 At each connected point, pick up a few threads and pull the thread across.
11 Trim the thread so that about 3 inches (7 cm) of thread remains.

12 Tie an overhand knot with the ends and pull the points together tightly. As each shape's points are pulled together they will form a puffy gather on the front side. Make sure excess fabric doesn't get caught between the points.
13 Knot two more times to secure. Trim so that about ½-inch (1 cm) remains.
14 Continue with the remaining sets of points until you have the pattern shown below.

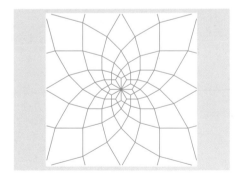

Shape the Shadowfold

15 Turn over and begin shaping the center dodecagon twist, flattening it in a clockwise direction.
16 The ring of triangles and squares will twist counterclockwise and clockwise, respectively.

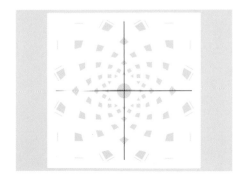

RADIATING ROSETTE, *continued*

17 The first ring that forms the rosette is the trickiest to fold. Lift the four intersecting pleats with your thumbs and forefingers and crease to form a trapezoid shape.

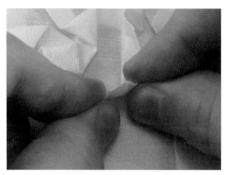

18 With your right forefinger, flip over the pleat on the right and lay the pleats from the two squares flat to the left. Tuck them underneath the top-layer trapezoid shape as you flatten them neatly onto one another.

19 Repeat Steps 17–18 for the remaining eleven points along the first ring.

20 The second, third, and fourth rings all pleat similarly. Lift the four intersecting pleats with your thumbs and forefingers and crease to form a trapezoid shape.

21 Lay the pleats flat towards the center while simultaneously tucking the pleats from the first ring underneath the second ring. Form two small triangles that extend past the top edge, forming neat points.

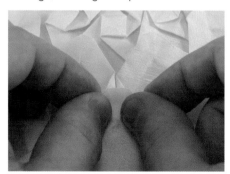

22 Repeat Steps 20–21 for the points along all of the remaining rings.

23 The final ring's pleats extend out to the edge of the fabric in two ways. In the middle of the square's edges, the two converging pleats should overlap each other slightly.

24 The converging pleats towards the corners of the square flatten by first extending the diagonal pleat.

25 Place your forefinger underneath the vertical pleat and then tuck the diagonal pleat under neatly to flatten.

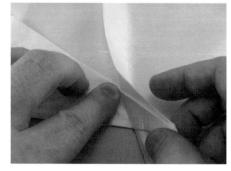

26 Repeat Steps 24–25 for the remaining pleats.

27 Iron the pleats gently, taking care to keep the underlying triangles neat and evenly extended. ∎

RADIATING ROSETTE PATTERN

▼ *Enlarge pattern to 200% of original size.*

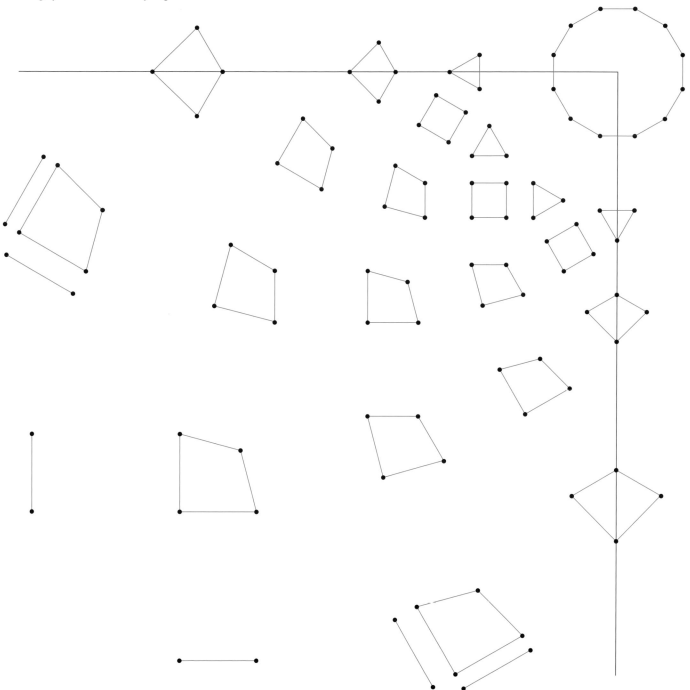

STAR OCTAGRAMS

Difficulty: 🏮🏮🏮 | *Size:* **18 × 18 inches** (46 × 46 cm)
Fabric: **39 × 39 inches** (99 × 99 cm) **of silk or linen**
Materials: **Needle, top-stitch thread, hand punch, pencil, iron, sewing machine, serger (optional)**

THE STAR OCTAGRAMS PATTERN CAN BE folded in a variety of ways. Although the sew folding is still straight-forward, some of the finished pleats are a bit more challenging. Those familiar with origami will recognize waterbomb bases and rabbit-ear folds used to flatten some of the pleats. This project, however, focuses on repeating the design in the lower-left-hand corner across the entire surface.

Prepare Cloth and Transfer Pattern

1 Enlarge the pattern on page 120 to 250% of original size, or download and print using the instructions on page 24.
2 Punch holes through the pattern at each marked circle.

3 Align the pattern's reflective lines, shown in pink, so their intersection is in the center of the fabric. Tape down to secure.
4 Mark each point using a pencil. *Double-check to be sure you've marked every point.*
5 Rotate the pattern 90°. Line up the shapes on the pink line. Tape down to secure.
6 Mark each point for the remaining quadrants of the fabric.
7 Remove the pattern and, using a pencil, lightly draw a line connecting the dots as shown on the pattern.
8 Hem or serge the edges about 1½–2 inches (4–5 cm) from the outermost dots on the pattern.

Start Sew Folding

9 Begin with each octagon twist. Pick up just a few threads of silk within one marked point. Draw your thread through, leaving about 3 inches (7 cm) of thread.
10 At each connected point, pick up a few threads and pull the thread across.
11 Trim the thread so that about 3 inches (7 cm) of thread remains.

12 Tie an overhand knot with the ends and pull the points together tightly. As each shape's points are pulled together they will form a puffy gather on the front side. Make sure excess fabric doesn't get caught between the points.
13 Knot two more times to secure. Trim so that about ½-inch (1 cm) remains.
14 Continue with the remaining sets of points until you have the pattern shown below.

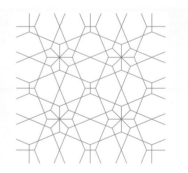

Shape the Shadowfold

15 Turn over and begin shaping all four octagonal twists clockwise.
16 Twist the centermost square, and all eight edge squares clockwise.
17 The square twists surrounding each octagonal twist will alternate

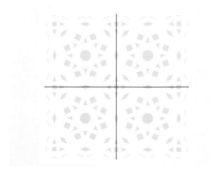

STAR OCTAGRAMS, *continued*

▶▶ *An advanced version of this project demonstrates that with only minor variations in the dot pattern it can then be folded to produce very different results.*

clockwise to counterclockwise. Locate any of the four corners of the Shadowfold and follow diagonally towards the nearest octagonal twist. The left-hand square will twist counterclockwise and the right-hand square will twist clockwise.

18 Alternate the directions of the remaining square twists surrounding the octagon. Repeat Steps 17–18 until all of the square twists are set in each quadrant.

19 Locate the initial square twists from Step 17. Raise the pleats between them and the octagonal twist. Press to a point and fold back down towards the octagon. Repeat for

the remaining sets of square twists *where the left-hand square twists counterclockwise and the right-hand square twists clockwise.* Continue for each quadrant.

20 Raise the remaining pleats from the octagons and the sets of squares *where the left-hand square twists clockwise and the right-hand square twists counterclockwise.* Press to a point and fold back down to the left, tucking the edge underneath the square twist.

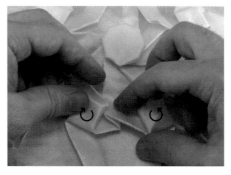

21 Just below the pleats made in Step 20, raise the intersection of the pleats forming an "X" and fold down towards the ring. Repeat for all sets.

22 Just below the pleats made in Step 19 raise the intersection. However, since the pleats from the square twists converge, neatly create small triangular flaps on both sides of the center, then fold down towards the ring. Press flat. Repeat for all sets.

23 The remaining pleats that surround the central and edge square twists complete the folding. Similar to the pleats made in Step 19, flatten each intersection. Be sure that the small square twists remain clockwise.

24 The edge pleats should be ironed so the entire Shadowfold lies flat. Gently iron the twists flat. Use steam to set if you made it from linen. ∎

ZILLIJ TABLECLOTH

Difficulty: 🔔🔔🔔 | *Size:* **Variable, depending on starting fabric**
Fabric: **Plain-woven tablecloth from a department store**
Materials: **Needle, top-stitch thread, hand punch, pencil, iron**

Making a Shadowfold tablecloth is just as simple as it was to make the Octagon Bedspread. By purchasing a factory-made round, oval, square, or rectangular tablecloth, you eliminate the need to find very wide cloth, or finish its edges. Choose a plain texture in any color. This project would look truly magnificent underneath glass atop a dining table.

Prepare Cloth and Transfer Pattern

1 Enlarge the pattern on page 121 to 450% of original size, or download and print using the instructions on page 24.
2 Punch holes through the pattern at each marked circle.
3 Find the center of your tablecloth by folding into quarters. Iron the layers and creases neatly.
4 Unfold, right side down, onto a large hard surface, such as a clean kitchen floor. Only the upper-right quarter needs to be perfectly flat at this time. However, if the edges hang off of a table, their weight might distort the fabric.
5 Align the pattern's vertical reflective line, shown in pink, along the creased line of the fabric. Make sure the center of the large decagon is at the center of the fabric. You might have to adjust the fabric underneath to "square it" with the pattern. Tape down to secure.
6 Mark each point using a pencil. *Double-check to be sure you've marked every point.*
7 Rotate the pattern 72° (one-fifth rotation) counterclockwise. Line up the pattern's sloping reflective line to the vertical position. Register the dots already marked through the holes in the pattern. Tape down to secure.
8 Mark each point using a pencil. *Double-check to be sure you've marked every point.*
9 Repeat three more times until the whole pattern has been transferred.
10 Remove the pattern and, using a pencil, lightly draw a line connecting the dots as shown on the pattern.

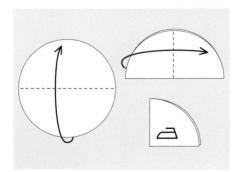

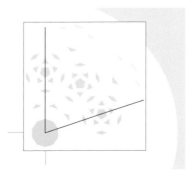

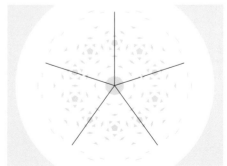

Start Sew Folding

11 Begin with the dodecagon twist. Pick up just a few threads of silk within one marked point. Draw your thread through, leaving about 3 inches (7 cm) of thread.

12 At each connected point, pick up a few threads and pull the thread across.

13 Trim the thread so that about 3 inches (7 cm) of thread remains.

14 Tie an overhand knot with the ends and pull the points together tightly. As each shape's points are pulled together they will form a puffy gather on the front side. Make sure excess fabric doesn't get caught between the points.

15 Knot two more times to secure. Trim so that about ½-inch (1 cm) remains.

16 Continue with the remaining sets of points until you have the pattern shown below.

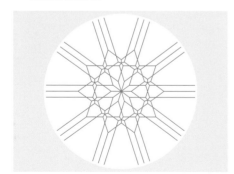

Shape the Shadowfold

17 Turn over and begin shaping the dodecagon twist and the 12 pentagon twists clockwise.

18 Lift a pleat radiating from the dodecagon twist and press the two layers together that form at each vertex that surrounds it.

19 Lay the pleat back down and press flat. Repeat for the remaining pleats.

20 Using the same method from Steps 18–19, flatten the pleats radiating from each of the pentagon twists.

21 Most of the remaining pleats are folded by raising the intersection of the pleats forming an "X." These connect the ring of stars with one another and connect the stars with the central flower. Just make the crease across each of the intersections. You will lay them flat in the next step.

22 Beginning with any star, lay the creases made in Step 21 down *away* from the pentagon twist. Proceed to the adjacent star and lay the creases *toward* the pentagon twist. Continue alternating in this way until all of the creases lie flat.

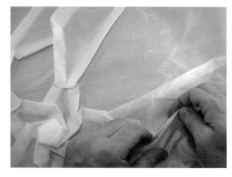

23 The pleats between each star that radiate to the edges of the fabric are made using the same method from Steps 18–19. Extend the parallel pleats out to the edges of the fabric.

24 Gently iron the entire Shadowfold flat. Use steam to set if necessary. You can see the hidden pattern in a similar design on page 9. ∎

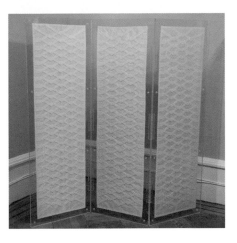

SCALES DIVIDER SCREEN

Difficulty: 🔔🔔🔔 | *Size:* **48 × 48 inches** (122 × 122 cm)
Fabric: **49½ × 89½ inches** (126 × 227 cm) **of silk**
Materials: **Needle, top-stitch thread, hand punch, pencil, iron, ruler, pins, sewing machine, acrylic and hardware** (see page 111)

THIS MODERN ADAPTATION OF THE SHOJI screen combines a simple pattern with minimalist mounting to showcase all aspects of a Shadowfold for interior design: translucent and opaque, and displaying both sides.

Although the Shadowfold scales design is very easy to make, precise pattern transfer, measurements, and finishing is required.

See page 111 for details on the acrylic materials and tools used to construct the frames.

Prepare Cloth and Transfer Pattern

1 Cut the fabric into three 16½ × 89½ inch (42 × 227 cm) rectangles.
2 Enlarge the pattern on page 122 to 170% of original size, or download

and print using the instructions on page 24.
3 Punch holes through the pattern at each marked circle.
4 Align the pattern's top reflective line, shown in pink, 2¼ inches (6 cm) from the top of the first fabric piece. Center the outermost dots between the fabric's sides. Tape down to secure.
5 Mark each point using a pencil, *except* for the dots encircled with green at the very top of the panel. *Double-check to be sure you've marked every point.*
6 Repeat the pattern seven more times by lining up the dots on the pink lines. Mark each point *except* for the dots encircled with orange at the

very bottom of the panel. Make sure you keep the pattern straight and centered as you go.
7 Remove the pattern and, using a pencil, lightly draw a line connecting the dots as shown on the pattern.

Start Sew Folding

8 Begin at the top and work down. Pick up just a few threads of silk within one marked point. Draw your thread through, leaving about 3 inches (7 cm) of thread.
9 At each connected point, pick up a few threads and pull the thread across.
10 Trim the thread so that about 3 inches (7 cm) of thread remains.
11 Tie an overhand knot with the ends and pull the points together tightly. As each shape's points are pulled together they will form a puffy gather on the front side. Make sure excess fabric doesn't get caught between the points.
12 Knot two more times to secure. Trim so that about ½-inch (1 cm) remains.
13 Continue with the remaining sets of points until you have the pattern shown on the next page.

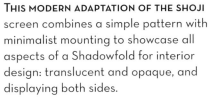

2¼ in (6 cm) **TOP**

BOTTOM

SCALES DIVIDER SCREEN, *continued*

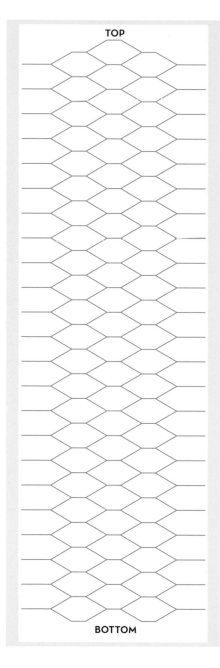

TOP

BOTTOM

Shape the Shadowfold

14 Turn over and begin shaping the triangular points. Start with the top-center point by lifting both layers with your thumbs and forefingers to crease the pleats together towards the tip.

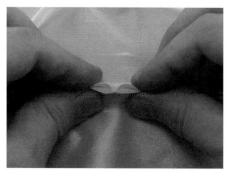

15 Insert your forefinger between the creases and, while pressing the top of the flaps against your thumbs, lay the entire point down flat. Extend the pleats out to the top edge of the fabric.

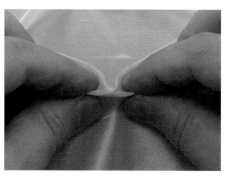

16 The second row forms two points. Repeat Steps 14–15, extending the outer pleats to the edges of the fabric.

17 The third row's pleats extend to the edges of the fabric. Tuck the pleat that travels upward underneath the pleat that travels downward. The resulting pleat will lie flat, perpendicular to the edges of the fabric. Repeat on the other side.

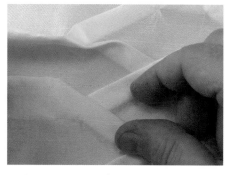

18 Repeat Step 17 for remaining rows, up to the last two rows.

19 The second-to-last row forms two points. Extend the outer pleats to the edges like you did for the second row.

20 The last row forms a single point. Tuck the fabric underneath the point to form a pleat that extends straight down to the bottom edge of the fabric.

21 Carefully iron all of the pleats. Start at the top and *slowly* reinforce each row, forming neat points and straight pleats.

22 Turn over and iron the back along the sides to firmly set those pleats. It's not necessary to iron the creases between the edges.

Hem the Edges of the Shadowfold

23 Trim the excess fabric formed by the diagonal pleats, along the edges near the top and bottom, to square all sides.

24 From the back, fold over ¾ inch (2 cm) along the left and right sides, slowly ironing as you go to keep the pleats neat and straight.

25 Tuck the raw edge underneath to form a rolled hem ⅜ inch (1 cm) wide, slowly ironing as you go to keep the pleats neat and straight.

26 Pin the edges at each row where the side pleats form thick layers.

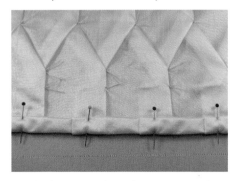

27 Machine sew the sides to secure the hem. Work slowly to be careful not to snag any pleats under the presser foot or the feed dogs.

29 Repeat Steps 24–27 to form a rolled hem on the top and bottom.

30 Make two more panels!

Make the Acrylic Frame

The materials you'll need to make the acrylic frame are:

- 6 pieces of ⅛-inch (3 mm) thick clear acrylic cut to 16×48 inches (41×122 cm)
- 6 acrylic hinges, 6 inches (15 cm) long
- 24 clear vinyl barrel nuts, ¼ inch (6 mm) long (metal barrel nuts may also be used, if desired)
- Tube of clear cement for acrylic (use the viscous tube-based kind rather than the liquid version)
- ¼-inch (6 mm) drill bit for acrylic (drill bits for acrylic are specially-designed for this material)
- Electric drill
- Small board and acrylic scrap to drill into and protect work surface
- Packing tape
- Ruler and pencil

The shop where you order the acrylic pieces to be cut will likely be familiar with the other specialty items. Leave the protective paper on the acrylic sheets for now.

31 Select two of the acrylic sheets. Tape the pair together securely with the packing tape.

32 Make a small dot with a pencil on the *short edge* of the acrylic on both sheets (not the face with the protective paper). Once the holes

are drilled, this will help you always keep the pairs matched.

33 Measure and mark the holes to be drilled. The corner marks are inset 1 inch (2.5 cm) from the edges. The middle marks are 16 inches (41 cm) from each of the corner marks.

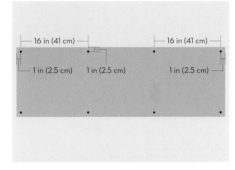

34 Underneath the first hole to be drilled, sandwich the acrylic scrap between the pair of taped sheets and a small wood board. The acrylic scrap will help prevent cracks as the drill bit exits the paired sheets.

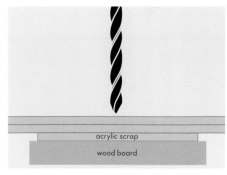

35 Press the sharp tip of the drill bit into the mark while also pressing hard with your other hand onto the sandwich to keep it together tightly.

36 Drill the hole straight through to the wood slightly. Repeat for the remaining holes.

37 Repeat Steps 31–36 on the remaining acrylic sheets. *However, mark the edges of the second set with two dots and the third set with three dots.*

38 Work on a surface with a protective cloth to prevent scratching the acrylic. Separate one of the pairs and lay out both sheets with their *outside* surfaces up. Remove the protective paper from this side.

39 Flip both sheets over with their *inside* surfaces up. Remove the protective paper.

40 With a lint-free cloth and glass cleaner, wipe the inside surfaces free of any dust and fingerprints.

41 Select one of the Shadowfold panels and check carefully for any dust or loose threads.

42 Lay out the panel, front side down, onto one of the acrylic sheets. Center within the array of drilled holes.

43 Flip the other sheet and lower it slowly onto the Shadowfold to sandwich it inside. If the Shadowfold shifts, gently lift an edge of the top sheet and nudge it to straighten.

44 Separate one of the barrel nuts and insert the barrel end up through a set of holes in any corner. Screw the post end into the barrel and tighten. Fasten the remaining corners, followed by the middle holes.

45 With a lint-free cloth and glass cleaner, wipe the outside surfaces free of any dust and fingerprints.

46 Repeats Steps 38–45 on the remaining acrylic sheets.

The screen is designed to open like an accordion and fold flat for convenience. This is accomplished by attaching hinges on one side between the first and second panels, and on the other side between the second and third panels. Use the diagram below as a guide to decide which orientation you prefer.

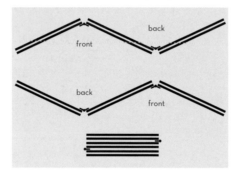

47 To affix the first set of hinges, lay two panels together side-by-side, with the fronts or backs facing up and sides touching.

48 Align the panels flush at the bottom so they will be level on the floor.

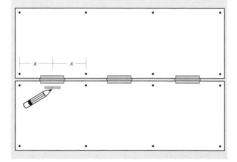

Gently slide the panel sides apart until the distance is equal between them, about ¼ inch (6 mm). *Note: This distance will vary slightly depending on the flat surface to be glued on the hinge's flange.*

49 Measure to find the center between a set of drilled holes. Mark on a piece of tape affixed outside of the area to be glued.

Caution: Using cement for acrylic will permanently mar unintended areas if any amount should accidentally get on the surface. It can be made much worse if you try to wipe it off. Use sparingly. The bond is very strong once cured.

50 Apply a thin bead of glue to each side of the hinge, keeping it at least ⅛ inch (3 mm) from any edges. This will allow it to spread between the surfaces without excess oozing out.

51 Very carefully invert the hinge and center it between the panels and the point marked on the tape. Press down for one minute to secure.

52 Repeats Steps 49–51 for the remaining two hinges. Allow to dry, in place, for at least 12 hours.

53 Flip the panels over and repeat Steps 48–52 for the third panel.

54 Fold the panels up before moving or storing them. ■

SHADOWFOLD SECRETS
Make each Shadowfold panel from different colored silk.

PATTERNS

PENTAGONAL STAR PILLOW PATTERN

▼ *Enlarge pattern to 147% of original size.*

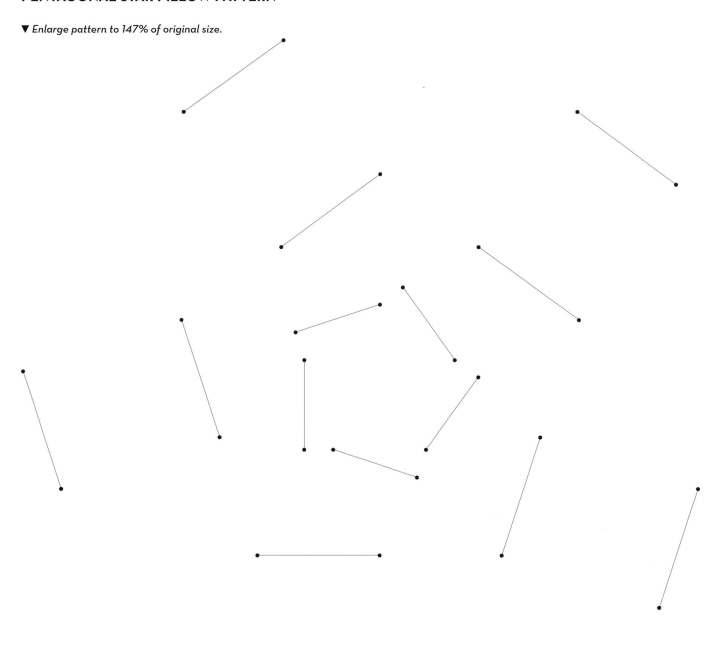

STAR-FLOWER PILLBOX HAT PATTERN

▼ *Do not enlarge pattern.*

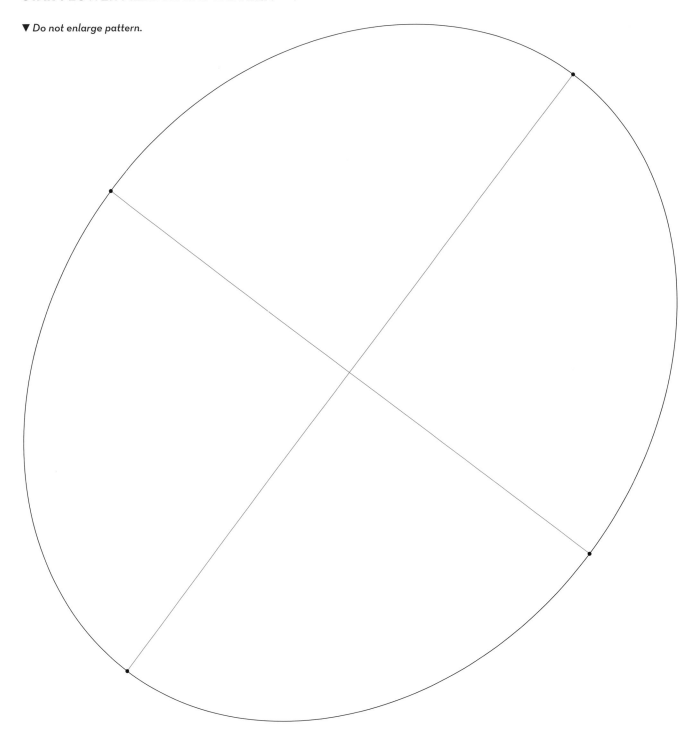

TWIST NECKTIE PATTERN

▼ *Enlarge pattern to 450% of original size.*

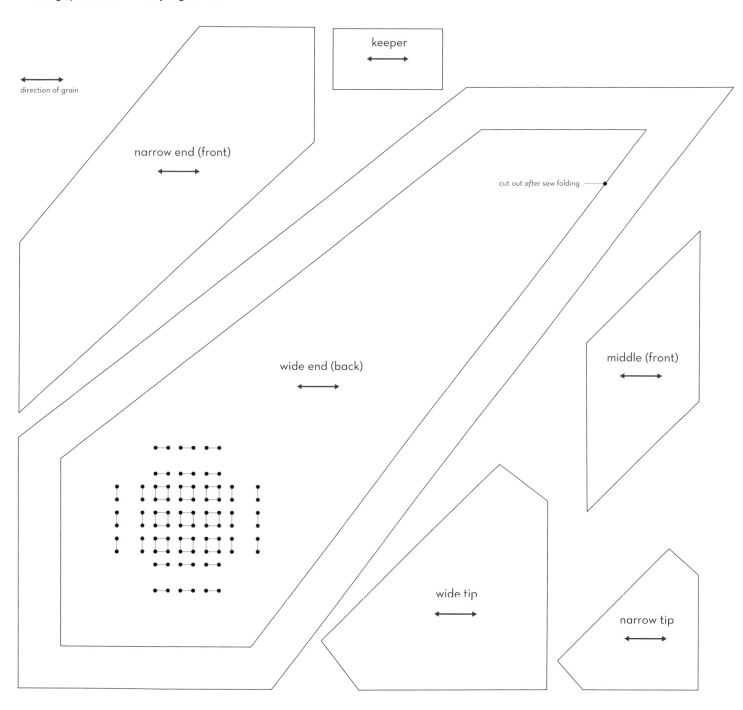

direction of grain

keeper

narrow end (front)

cut out *after* sew folding

wide end (back)

middle (front)

wide tip

narrow tip

PINWHEEL PATH LAMP PATTERN

▼ ▶▶ *Enlarge pattern to 286% of original size.*

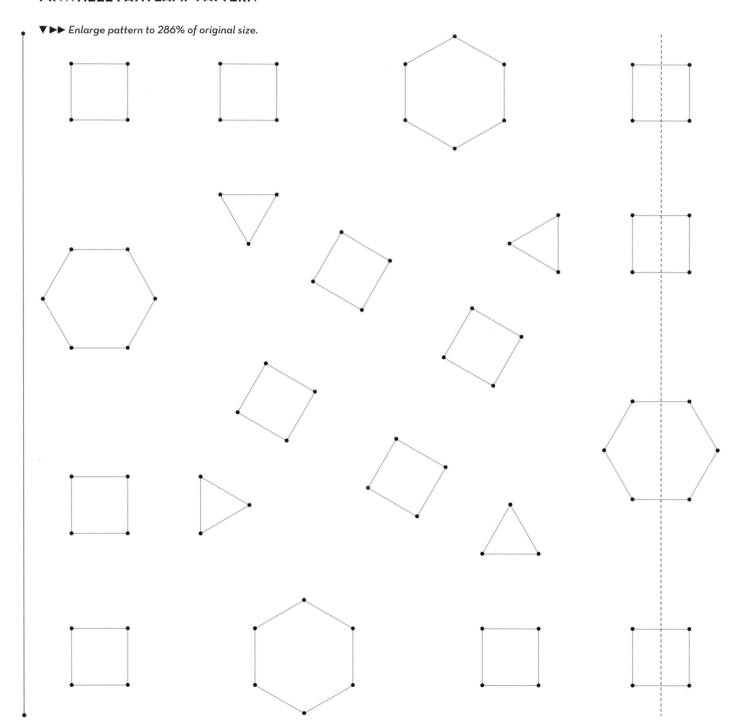

PINWHEEL PATH LAMP PATTERN

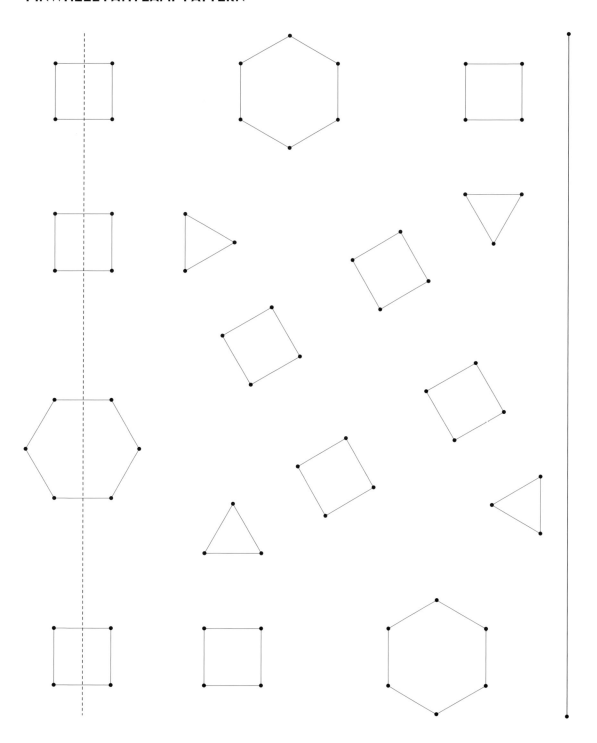

▼ *Enlarge pattern to 250% of original size.*

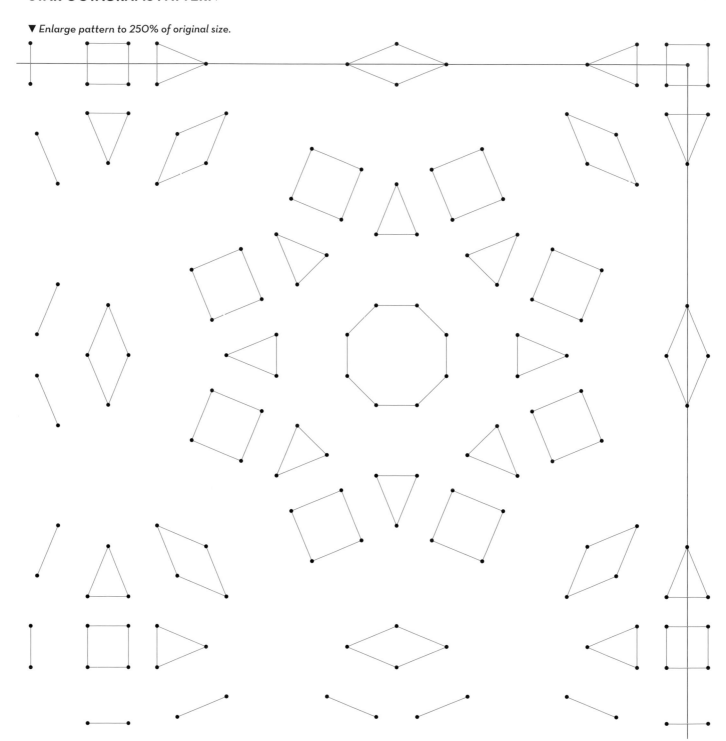

ZILLIJ TABLECLOTH PATTERN

▼ *Enlarge pattern to 450% of original size.*

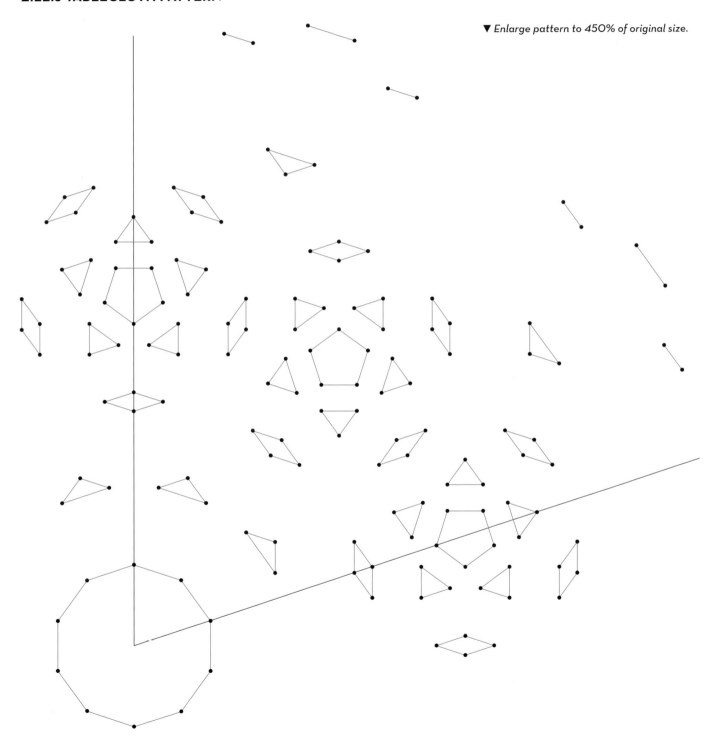

SCALES DIVIDER SCREEN PATTERN

▼ *Enlarge pattern to 170% of original size.*

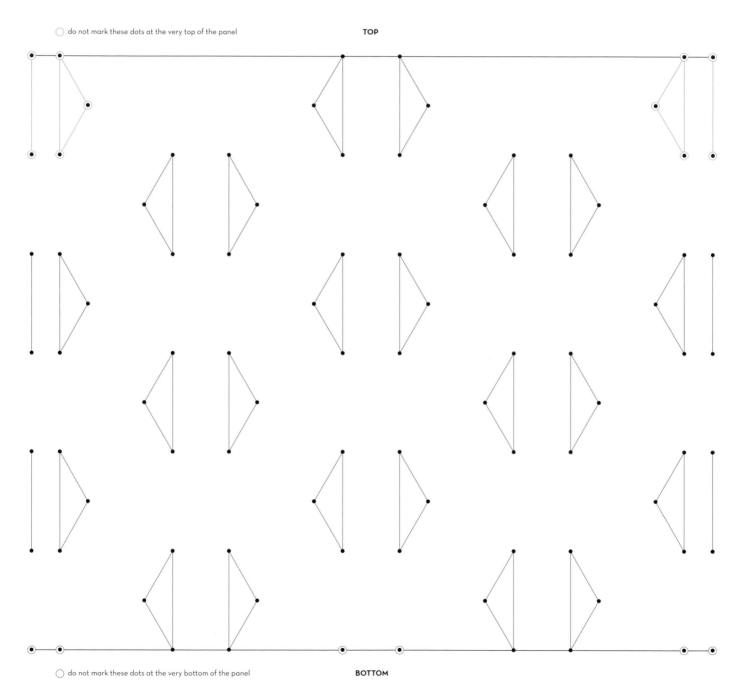

do not mark these dots at the very top of the panel

TOP

do not mark these dots at the very bottom of the panel

BOTTOM

RESOURCES

FABRIC

USA

Mood Designer Fabrics
225 West 37th Street
New York, New York 10018
1 212 730 5003
www.moodfabrics.com

Mood Designer Fabrics
6151 West Pico Boulevard
Los Angeles, California 90035
1 323 653 6663
www.moodfabrics.com

Britex Fabrics
146 Geary Street
San Francisco, California 94108
1 415 392 2910
www.britexfabrics.com

Fishman's Fabrics
1101 South Desplaines Street
Chicago, Illinois 60607
1 312 922 7250
www.fishmansfabrics.com

Vogue Fabrics
718–732 Main Street
Evanston, Illinois 60202
1 847 864 9600
www.voguefabricsstore.com

Jo-Ann Fabric & Craft Stores
Retail stores in more than 30 states
1 888 739 4120
www.joann.com

UK

MacCulloch & Wallis
25–26 Dering Street
London W1S 1AT
02 07 629 0311
www.macculloch-wallis.co.uk

AUSTRALIA

Silk Gallery Fine Fabrics
178 High Street
Kew VIC 3101
61 03 98550622
www.silkgallery.com.au

JAPAN

These Web sites are in Japanese only:

Yuzawaya
www.yuzawaya.co.jp

Tomato
www.nippori-tomato.com

ACRYLIC

USA

T & T Plastic Land, Inc.
315 Church Street
New York, New York 10013
1 212 925 6376
www.ttplasticland.com

Canal Plastics Center
345 Canal Street
New York, New York 10013
1 212 925 1666
www.canalplasticscenter.com

TAP Plastics, Inc.
154 South Van Ness Avenue
San Francisco, California 94103
1 415 864 7360
www.tapplastics.com

Ridout Plastics
5535 Ruffin Road
San Diego, California 92123
1 800 474 3688
www.eplastics.com

Petersen Brothers Plastics
2929 North Pulaski Road
Chicago, Illinois 60641
1 773 286 5666
www.petersenplastics.com

UK

Acrylic Design
3A/3B Shakespeare Industrial Estate
Shakespeare Street
Watford
Hertfordshire WD24 5RS
01 92 324 1122
www.acrylicdesign.co.uk

C & A Building Plastics
Bidder Street
London E16 4ST
02 07 474 0474
www.casupply.co.uk

Barkston, Ltd.
Unit 11
Bridgewater Road
Riverside Place
Leeds LS9 0RQ
www.theplasticpeople.co.uk

Colmac Plastic Fabricators
Unit C1 (up)
Southway
Bounds Green Industrial Estate
Bounds Green
London N11 2UL
02 08 361 4807
www.colmacplastics.co.uk

AUSTRALIA

Plastral
370 Darebin Road
Thornbury VIC 3071
61 39 490 0111
www.plastral.com.au

LAMP PARTS

USA

Texas Lamp Manufacturing
505 East Highway 80
Forney, Texas 75126
1 972 564 5267
www.txlampparts.com

Art Wire Works
5401 West 65th Street
Chicago, Illinois 60638
1 708 458 3993
www.artwireworks.com

IKEA
www.ikea.com

CRAFT SUPPLIES

USA & CANADA

Michaels Stores, Inc.
Over 500 retail stores in more
than 49 states and Canada
1 800 642 4235
www.michaels.com

INDEX

ADDITIONAL PHOTO CREDITS
Photos copyright by their creator.

ACKNOWLEDGMENTS

From Jeffrey Rutzky

This book was finally made possible because of my good friend, Chris K. Palmer. He trusted me with his wealth of designs and techniques, knowing I could bring Shadowfolds to a wide audience.

I am very grateful to our publisher, Kodansha America, and especially Laura Shatzkin and Tomoe Sumi, for immediately recognizing the potential for this work.

Thank you to our team, with whom I've worked for many years on my previous origami and papercraft books. Ruth O'Brien, our editor, contributed her crafting expertise as well as her words. And Mark A. Gore and Lynne Yeamans produced beautiful photographs of the projects. Thank you also to Sharyn Rosart and Quirk Packaging for allowing us to use their offices to shoot in.

Nathaniel Marunas (who has taught me everything I know in publishing) continues to be supportive of every move I make in writing, designing, and producing craft books.

Several folding friends have been helpful and inspirational: Eric Gjerde, Robert J. Lang, Paul Jackson, David Brill, Polly Verity, Jerry Marciniak, and Jean-Charles Trebbi.

Thanks to my mother, I learned to sew before I could fold. And my father would have been extremely proud of this book.

Most of all, however, I am indebted to my wife, Nanci, for all of her love and support. She certainly deserves to have her favorite fold, the Peace Purse!

From Chris K. Palmer

Thanks to my friend and collaborator Jeff Rutzky. Without his unwavering support, encouragement, and love for my art, and his excellent skill and hard work to produce this book, it would still be in the "cave" of my studio.

I am grateful more than words can say to Shuzo Fujimoto-sensei for his warm encouragement to follow in his footsteps.

I am thankful for friendships with Tomoko Fuse, Makoto Yamaguchi, Toshikazu Kawasaki, and Jun Maekawa. They made my relationship with Fujimoto-sensei possible. Their works inspire me and their generosity make my experiences in Japan truly special.

I am indebted to Jeremy Shafer for his joyful enthusiasm, for going where no one had gone before, and for first breaking the ice and inspiring me to make the leap from paper to textiles.

Thanks to David Rodriguez whose vision and hard work first brought Shadowfolds to the fashion world.

My students who became friends—Jerry Marciniak and Ushio Ikegami—have been a great help in developing how to teach and present this work.

Thanks to Nellie Dorn, whose postcard brought me to the Alhambra. Many thanks to David Gottlieb, Hans and Christian Nielsen, Michael LaFosse, Richard Alexander, and Kate and Richard Jones; all generously supported me for many years as I mastered this medium.

Most importantly I am grateful for the love from my family: John, Stephanie, and Joanna. My greatest masterpieces were created surrounded by the warm glow of their hearth.

By

Vineyard Light

poems by ROSE STYRON
photographs by CRAIG DRIPPS

introductions by GEORGE PLIMPTON
and PETER SACKS

RIZZOLI
NEW YORK

For our youngest, Alexandra,
and for my mother, Selma, and the kin between:
lovers of the Vineyard, all.

—R.S.

To the memory of Virginia Kranz Crossland.

—C.D.

First published in the United States of America in 1995 by
Rizzoli International Publications, Inc.
300 Park Avenue South, New York, New York 10010

Copyright © 1995 by Rizzoli International Publications, Inc.
Poems copyright © 1995 by Rose Styron
Photographs copyright © 1995 by Craig Dripps
Reprinted in paper, 2002

Library of Congress Cataloging-in-Publication Data

Styron, Rose.
    By vineyard light : poems and photographs of Martha's
Vineyard / poems by Rose Styron ; photographs by Craig
Dripps ; foreword by George Plimpton ; introduction by
Peter Sacks.

        p.   cm.

    HC ISBN 0-8478-1871-3; PB ISBN 0-8478-2491-8

    1. Martha's Vineyard (Mass.)--Poetry. 2. Martha's
Vineyard (Mass.)--Pictorial works. I. Dripps, Craig. II. Title.
PS3569.T89B9 1995   94-43022
811'.54--dc20   CIP

Designed by Nicky Lindeman and Mirko Ilić

Printed in China

TABLE OF CONTENTS

ABOUT THE PHOTOGRAPHS

Craig Dripps is a teacher by profession—he has taught for more than twenty years at Haverford School, a boys' prep school in Pennsylvania, where he is the chairman of the math department. This has allowed him to spend his summers in Martha's Vineyard, where he has pursued his passions for music composition and photography.

He came to photograph by the usual route: at the age of ten or so he was given a box camera with a viewing lid that flipped up. One afternoon during his high school days, he took a picture of a scenic spot on the island—E. B. Keith's pond, a stretch of crystal edged with great oaks and populated with geese (though now, sadly, its water is murky and overgrown with sedge and marsh grasses). Something about his picture of Keith's pond in its pristine days spurred his interest in photography; since those days, graduating from his box camera to a Canon 35 mm, he has gone on taking pictures with considerable success.

From his earliest days, Dripps's subjects were invariably *things* rather than people. His family noticed, and indeed Craig's father made a point of populating *his* photographs with family and friends—"filling a void" as he put it. In the present volume, as readers will discover, the human presence is only occasionally evident in Craig's pictures: a workman in a boat yard, a couple of skinny kids leaping off a sea-bound boulder, a pair of young girls on an amusement park slide, two fishermen, one simply a reflection of the fisherman in the water, as if at the last the camera eye had turned away from humankind. The *works* of man are evident enough—the sweet symmetry of sailboats lined up on a beach, a dory (could someone be lying down out of sight, taking a snooze on the duckboards?), a lighthouse, a beach shack, a gazebo in a winter landscape, an empty hammock strung between two trees, graveyards, the occasional grazing horse, boats at their moorings, an empty macadam road—it is almost as if the photographer felt that the corporeal presence of humankind would shatter the spell of these places.

the fact is that Craig does most of his camera work when very few people are around. He is up at first light, long before the island population stirs in its beds, and thus for four hours or so "the Vineyard is basically mine," he says. He knows every cranny of the island as if he were its designated surveyor. One of the reasons he is so knowledgeable is that he often tutors math in the summer months, traversing the island to the homes of his young charges like a country doctor making calls—carrying with him a schoolbag of marked papers along with his camera.

A summer or so ago I went to hear Rose Styron read her poems in a small gallery where Craig Dripps's photographs were displayed. The room in which Rose sat at one end was packed with listeners, many of them sitting on the floor. Indeed the place was so crowded that, having arrived late, I kept to the adjacent room and wandered about looking at the photographs. The day was warm, and the wide doors of the barnlike gallery were open to a soft summer breeze. I could hear Rose's voice in the next room and the occasional odd sighlike *umm* sound that listeners make when a poem is done. It was my first summer on the Vineyard. I had been taken to many of the scenic views I was looking at in the photographs— Windy Gates and its cliffs, Black Point, Menemsha and its fishing boats, Squibnocket Pond, the West Chop lighthouse, the West Tisbury Oak—and to see these places in the photographs, illuminated by what Rose was reciting in the other room, was to go through a kind of refresher course on the island.

One of the tests of a great photograph is that it tells you something about a familiar scene that you had not noticed before—not necessarily anything specific, but perhaps a mood, or a feeling. How fortuitous that Craig Dripps's photographs and Rose Styron's poetry—to which the same test can be successfully applied—have been combined in this volume: a perfect marriage of word and image.

George Plimpton

ABOUT THE POETRY

Among its other attributes, art may be one of the oldest yet most renewable means by which we can attach ourselves to a place, and thereby to the world. In the poems of Rose Styron, as in the photographs of Craig Dripps, the place is the island of Martha's Vineyard—lit, framed, and focused by the resources of poetry itself. With a versatile grace that shifts between disarming snapshots and longer exposures, her poems bring the reader within touching distance of an "antique landscape / rubbed by hand," and within musing distance of our "mysterious connection with the night, the deep, the shore."

"You come too," Robert Frost wrote in one of his early pastoral poems. Styron's invitation is implicit in her directly shared responses to islandscapes that are at once familiar yet freshly seen: the coves, the meadows, the light-filled bays and beaches, the stone walls and wildflowers, the drifting mist or shine, the sometimes eerie calm that edges toward menace as a storm comes in or a season turns away. Such scenes are offered deftly and lucidly, in words that may startle us to a new alertness, provide us with a verbal island of meditation, or shape an impression that would otherwise have eluded our senses or slipped from memory. So too, here are poems that reawaken an innocence and openness to charm that we might otherwise have lost forever. A deliberately naive rhyme, a lilt and cadence, a fanciful play of associations (stars and minnows, South Beach and shimmering porcelain), all become means of cherishing the world and the perceiver, the sweet motion of the leaves as well as the continuing desire of whoever finds that motion sweet. To dream, to fear, to regret, to let go, to rejoice, to wish again: as if they were inner regions, such capacities are honored here no less than the physical places of the island that bring them forth or that seem to respond to their calling S.

But there is still more to find among these lines, such as the images of friendship, of family linkages, and of the sense that "no man is an island" any more than the Vineyard, despite its relative seclusion, is cut off from what happens across the waters. For Rose Styron, much of whose life continues to be actively committed to the international cause of human rights, the place-names Tashmoo, Menemsha, Vineyard Haven, may find themselves alongside Belfast, Cartagena, Prague. A moment of rural tranquillity may refine an ethical as much as an aesthetic perspective. The sight of a horse grazing through a stone-piled wall may evoke the image of alterable barriers elsewhere in the world—barriers no less between aspiration and reality, comfort and risk, deprivation and fulfillment.

Like the low stone walls that crisscross the island, or skeins of light across the waters and grasses, more motifs ripple through this collection than can be mapped by a casual tour. For that reason these poems and photographs will reward revisiting as they develop associations between each other as well as between the two mediums. One of the strongest yet most delicate motifs to emerge is that of time and its passages. Whether it is dawn, evening, or midnight, or the seasons like strange ferries in their rhythms of arrival and departure, the poems attune such passages of outer time to the inner seasons of youth and aging, of birthdays, weddings, and memorials, of renewals and backward glances. While knowing "how swiftly the starry minnows / disappear," or how summer laughter may echo into a wintry farewell "for us all / departing," the poet has the gift of making what is fleeting linger as it departs. It is a gift deepened by the poetic equivalent of time-lapse photography, an etching of repeated journeys from spring to fall. Styron's gift, complete with gleanings of spiritual intuition, thus becomes as much one of time as it is of place and its hallowing. And through the medium of her words, like the "silvered hay" of that "antique landscape / rubbed by hand," it is in this harvest of poems, of an island, of parts of a life, that we can receive that gift, keep it with us, carry it away.

Peter Sacks

No one's awake
but us, and a bird.
The day's too beautiful
to speak a word.

This antique landscape   rubbed by hand   shines through the mist   K   like silvered hay
                                                                         A
                                                                         T
its hewn rail fence   greyed barn, sweet fields   where dusty birds hide   A   startled, focus day.
                                                                         M
                                                                         A

Wedding Prelude

I

At Brookside Farm the oxen graze
tilting their horns as harriers glide
aslant the wind, homeward.
The weathered oxcart unused rests
against the welcoming barn.

II

At Brookside Farm the oxen gaze
not from dark-hollowed sockets
mouths agape at ongoing Guernicas.
No masters hanged from the roadsign cross,
no choirboys hidden in chestnut trees,
leaves of midsummer plunging all
around them. No skies spray ash or
blackened rivers bone-full overflow.

III

At Brookside Farm the oxen gaze
on dappled horses—roan, grays—
munching the feathered hillside.
Their gilded tails swat flies,
remembered stars.

From great verandah chairs
the cats uncurl, lions yawning
in their wicker lairs
as I walk by a greener century—
the tumbled birdhouse,
half-tamed pastures, theirs.

IV

What is perfection
but a sudden gate—low, white
in the long stone wall that
frames an English garden?

Three horses, strolling over now
to watch me enter,
nibble an escaping waterfall of blooms
behind the latticed arbor.
Wild turkeys flap beyond them
up into the heavy branches to observe
whatever ceremony.

V

I hesitate, my sleeve
caught on a thorny gatepost vine
of private history, recent untidy dream.
Could it have been this very gate,
affairs ago, unguarded? Then
tarrying inside, bees charging
the blossoms and the laden grass,
I frantic sought for some stone cleft
behind the arbor, a contained escape
to wilderness, and, looking back
from familiar fields
one dreamless morning, pardon.

Foxglove, ageratum, lupine, somnolent
rose I must have planted in my sleep
border the wall again within, unshadowed.
All May, forgetting to rehearse, I'd lie
rabbit alert in the uncut grass.

Green joys tangled my ears.
Nearby crows still ripped the earth for worms
but not a fatal wing whirred past.
Ready for formality again, the wall
surveyed, I heed annunciation.

VI

Whatever ceremony, it shall begin
at four o'clock, surprising as the sky
that clears, the winds that rise
to honor such occasions. The light at four
has followed me through the seasons,
crashing stone-spread clouds
in quicksilver County Clare, arrowing
the cave I shared with hermit crabs
under the clay-dried cliff at Windy Gates,
pacing St. Lucia's rim,

just as the mourning doves that circled
my youth followed me isle to isle
when the steamship pulled away
from Plato's harbor. I would face
those saints and oracles alone
but for the doves' discreet antiphony.
Or as Orion, night after night
so far and dark I sometimes fear to
breathe, holds out his starry sword-edge,
sign: protection. The light at four
returns to the strict garden and
the runaway fields
where goslings waddle to their newborn
pond and turkeys glimpsed at daybreak
balance like rusty gypsies in the tree.

VII

Punctual as light, framed in the center
doorway of romance—the farmhouse
white-trimmed, shingled gray, high
windows that fit his pilgrim heritage
and the windmill standing by—
Zen godfather, freshly ironed
into his oriental robes,
becomes our minister of afternoon.

An hour ago in khaki shorts,
peeled alpine boots, he sent me
scavenging a plant stand
for the stone wall altar, placed
three unmatched bowls for offerings,
and picked a columbine, a bellflower
for the cruet vase.
Unravelling the woodsy-odored cord
from Mary's drawer, he fashioned
delicate whisks from the attentive
pine branch. All concentration,
having touched so lightly
the young bridegroom on his shoulder
with tanned fingers, he is ready,
haloed as our tallest elm
after the hurricane sheared past,
to guide our celebration.

VIII

Groom, godfather—my dearest son, my friend—
I watch you both on Captain Flanders' path,
dragonflies stitching the organdy air,
mayblooms knotting each thread
of tension and affection between us
into a bridal veil you walk beneath,
the puritan winter melted, the slope
and damp stone wall gathering
light for us at four o'clock, gathering
our kin, all children from our past, into
this wedding.

PAINTED SCREEN

Through Chinese screens

rosewood and the pale silk fabric

we call sky

a pure white heron over the water

doubles our reflection:

the artist is responsible

for God, responsible to man.

for God, responsible to man.

the artist is responsible

doubles our reflection:

a pure white heron over the water

we call sky

rosewood and the pale silk fabric

Through Chinese screens

GOODNIGHT, GREAT SUMMER SKY

Goodnight, great summer sky
world of my childhood and the star-struck sea.

White chaise from that ancestral southern
porch my raft,
white goose-down quilt my ballast,
under Orion on the green-waved lawn
I float, high—
new moon, old craft
tide strong as ever to the sheer horizon.

Over the seawall, on the dock
Andromeda their strict and jeweled guard
as tall Orion—seas and lawns ago—

chose to be mine,
our children sleep: Alexandra, Tom
under their folded goose-wing sails
true friends in dream,
the folly wrangle of their sibling day
outshone by starlight.

Calm island evening, never-ending sea—
our lovers' rages, too, are quiet,
drowned.

Miracle of midsummer, the trust of dark
sails us beyond this harbor.

R
A
I

N

Three days rain
or years

the pond at night
a foreign constellation

fireflies before June
new treble frogs

white lilac blooming
I never knew before

at the far end of stillness
the dam's steady rain

willow in the mist
shadow of pale moons

the silhouette of enormous
ferns and hollow trees

in the close alley
under my skin's feet

wet pine needles
pebbles

the first call of death.

Gale

TOMORROW, WHEN WINTER LUCK'S
FALLEN, SAY
MY GRAVE-FINE FEATHERER,
"TARRED YOUR WAY."

WHEN I HAVE SUNG FROM ME
WILLOW AND WING
FLUNG AND STUNG FROM ME
FIDDLE OF DOVES
SUCH SORROW MAY SHUDDER ME,
WORN, ON HER STRING
TARNISH, TRANQUIL ME
DRY IN HER GLOVES
AND DOWN BE MY
SOUNDER DAY.

NOW, CHARM TO THE COPPERY
AUTUMN-NIGHT GALE
SWUNG HIGH AT THE STAR-WASTING
TIDE-WHITE SAIL
LET ME SHINE WITH MY LOVES!

OCEAN PARK

Empty gazebo in the snow-vast gardens
no indigo concert for a sailor's moon
no prince and jester
    conspiring laughter
the lanterned pageant gone.

Where is Oak Bluffs but on maps of summer?
The bugle tapestry, the fireworks hymn
image and echo
    imprint the cold sky
daring our year begin.

Lil's

January.
Ice on the jetty.
Stones blacker than wet
slates after school.
The scary
waters of winter
have given up their feint,
splintered, are still.

At Lil's
a fire, not her roses as I thought
at first, breaks from the windows,
spreads next door
and soon to every easterly
windowpane on shore
as the new ferry
shanghais us out of the harbor.

A memory of Dash
tall and furious glows
and half-blown footprints fill
paths to the beach, the jetty,
crazy forgotten lobster pot
and frozen gull
and laughter, Lil's

across the water
like a final uncomplicated wish
for us all
departing,
echoes echoes echoes
fragile January.

SEPTEMBER, AND THE SHENANDOAH

FANTASY OF BRIGANTINES

SAILS TO WINDWARD, GRANDLY

DOWN THE REAL HORIZON POINTS HER PROW

AND DISAPPEARS. IN VINEYARD HAVEN

WE, BEREFT ON DOCKS AND LAWNS,

DREAM A LAST VOYAGE, WATCH HER GO

TAKING SUMMER WITH HER, NOW.

SHENANDOAH

EACH CRISP AUTUMN

Each crisp autumn

there are fewer leaves, more clarity—

light cycles of the haymound

odors of late roses

rivers rushing where we

once meandered

content in the casual chaos of each

season, plotting no espionage

because we did not know

the world as terror then.

Death and a Wilderness of Dreams

Death and a wilderness of dreams
pursue my waking.

I have no poem for you this morning
only surprise at friendship and farewell—
the smoky trajectories of stars
echo such music.

Outside my tender cabin
where the wings from evening's butterfly
shone on the windowed midnight edge
of the sharpest crescent moon

shimmering grass belongs to the robins
a white-tailed deer nibbles the garden
ancient lilies open the lake anew.

All my earthly provinces being spoken for,
also my children, my mind empty by way of fullness
is ready for sunrise as the lightening sky.

Death and a wilderness of dreams
pursue my waking
but I am gone.

Trajectories

Déjà vu: I am undone again
by deadline and farewell. Half-
formed questions for the disappearing
dry on my lips, escape my fingers.
Stars I caught a tune from
that first rising
echo no music. Grandfather dandelion,
the dawn moon fades, stranding
my feathers in a meadowed sky
so I must walk from yesterday's
estates to Vineyard Sound, out
into the waves of my unclaimed dreams.

How long can the adventures of a high-
flown season—renaissance in Budapest,
Belfast on the edge, that shining
fermentation, Cartagena's,
keep me from sinking? Tucked
in my matted pocket, salty, limp,
are all the maps of spring.
August wakens me to winglessness
so far from shore.

I float a while
on memory, the hymns of shorebirds.
I hear the roseate tern versing
the light clouds, sail to Gay Head:

     Most lucent bird, thou roseate tern
     white, black-scarfed, saucy
     feathers preened
     smile at your offspring
     nestled in the sand. And if
     the osprey's safely on his perch
     no strangers near, be Zen-of-mind
     and chance an elegant stroll
     along that strand.

No Zen mind here, but still
I watch a subtler creature
stray toward our harbor. Whimbrel,
willet, curlew, who you are
is less important on the dazzled tide
than purity of tone, the sense
I stretch for as you pass. . . .

OCTOBER HARBOR

A POSSE OF GULLS ON OUR DOCK.
ALREADY OCTOBER PREYS
FAT, MULTIPLE, STRONGBEAKED
WITHOUT THE SUN. NO COLORS ONLY SHADES
PATROL THE CLAWS OF BREAKERS.

WHERE CAN IT LIE, THAT FRAGILE LATE SPRING
MORNING, BUOYS CHIMING ON THE BLUE WIND,
THE BAY A SHIMMER OF BELL GLASS
WE'D FOLLOW TO THE SOUND?

WHERE THE SQUALL ENDS
AGAIN I KNOW
ISLANDS, ORCHARDS, REEFS
WILL DISAPPEAR BENEATH YOUR SAIL'S AURORA.

GULLS, GATHERERS OF THE CLAN
RETURNED, FORGIVEN, SHINING NOW
STAND FAST TO WEB ME
FOOTLOOSE PRISONER HERE.

FORGOTTEN GRAVEYARD

Forgotten graveyard sheared by light
this quiet morning of surprise
shimmers with souls from English poems
that roused us each
in clarion days of childhood.

      Now on West Chop Rise
where we slow-waking walk past night
inhaling summer—a lighthouse rose,
blossoms tumbling by a pasture gate—
before the politics and rhymes
of noon define us

         faces once close tease.
Light through the fence intensifies
and this desire: no midday come,
I in that corner by the ancient stone
shadowed
       again, alone
the world going by all afternoon.

      I do not mean forever.
Given
choices for home or the farther climb
tomorrow some bright road I'd choose,
friendship and walking on.

GREEN GAMES

Heart of the island, this centuried oak
green-crusted octopus bared as we chase
last leaves down the windtunnel streets of November
beats in our winter limbs
strong as the memory of sea.

Inland the children curl slow over strategems,
gravity's cities. Come June may they wake
to imagine-remember swift climbs and green games
in its branches, seize
summer's simplicity.

WEST
TISBURY'S FAIR

the ferris wheel is going up
the carousel and little cars
are getting ready for my ride
around the earth and to the stars

puppies and ponies at the fence
fiddles, aromas on the air—
what summer prize might I win tonight
in paradise, West Tisbury's Fair?

BLUES

Fishing for blues
from the afternoon jetty
the man of our dreams
takes a god's silhouette.

By eventide casting
his lifeline arcs, glitters
against this blackness.
The moon's minaret

(a lighthouse at sunset
winged raptors around it
its beam through reluctant
darks circling us home)

has caught him believing
in the power of midnight
our starry souls
scattering the foam.

Fisherman

MILES SOUTH AND OUT OF GAY HEAD
WEST PAST MENEMSHA BIGHT
WASQUE SILVER CHANNELS EAST
RIFFS NORTH AND ICY SOUND

THROUGH TURNER'S RADIANT SEA HAZE
VERMEER'S LATE DELFT BLUE LIGHT
ON CHARCOAL BAY OR BLEACHED LAGOON
OR MERCURY-MIRRORED POND

A LONE BOAT'S CASTING, TROLLING,
RIDING ANCHOR, SILENT, SKILLED—
LUCK'S WARRIOR, ISLAND FISHERMAN
BEHOLDEN NOW TO NONE

THUS HERO TO US MORTALS, THRALLS
TO SKY AND SHORES WE'VE WILLED.
HIS MYSTERY: WORK,
ADVENTURE, LOVE ARE ONE.

Good-bye Strict Shores

Good-bye strict shores!
The sea's upon me.
I am gone
into a wilderness of waves.
The sky showers
incessant minnows.
The mud nourishes
my seaweed shroud.
The water's breath
in my breathless space
blows green as the stems
of Queen Anne's lace,
sweet as the motion
of leaves, desire
that led me early here.

How swiftly the starry minnows
disappear.

VINEYARD LIGHT

To live in a lighthouse,
cloud islands by
the tide lazing in
the steamer's farewell
the tall ship's sail
against sunset fires
as dusk descends
a Thanksgiving sky

awaiting snowfall
as you and I
await desire's
white harvest

to walk the fields
where wildflowers shone
(fog waves its wand:
the trees, the sand
seawall and spectrum
landscapes gone)

when the world invites us
to disappear
the foghorn hollows
a cave of air
and the lighthouse beam
like a soul's high flare
illuminates God
first there, now here

inside: safe midnight
fog at seven
we still unclaimed
by the buoy's clanging
the bustle of town
the arriving ferry

high in our stairclimbed
crystal aerie
the foghorn intoning
heaven
to live in a lighthouse
or just nearby
was childhood's dream.

ISLAND WOODS

Come walk with me
in the West Chop Woods
when the sun has burned the sand,
wild breakers batter
our fishing rocks
or the streets to town are jammed.

Walk barefoot along
its earth-soft trails
overhung with oak and pine.
Let your pup chase squirrels
or surprise a grouse
where the huckleberry bushes shine.

Or come next May
when the fern spreads green
and the lady's slipper first uncurls
and the white pole risen
at the wood's far edge
its American flag unfurls.

Beyond this kingdom
the lighthouse waits
fairways and the tide-ride shore,
but the path disappearing
at the fallen tree here
is one we must explore.

A cardinal's flash,
a monarch's flare,
through sky-frames the arrowed geese—
come walk with me
in the West Chop Woods
on our many trails to peace.

MORNING PLACES

WILD INVITATION
AT THE CLOSED WHITE GATE

TAMED STALLION GRAZING
THROUGH A STONE-PILED WALL

ROSARIES OF BIRD SONG
COUNT THE EARLY LIGHT

AS OLD BARRIERS ALTER
UNDER SUMMER'S BLOOM

IN CHILMARK
IN CAPETOWN, LHASA, PRAGUE, ALL

THE MORNING PLACES
CLAIMED TOO LONG BY DREAM.

A STRANGER'S BEACH

A stranger's beach, trespassed in December
Draws all the skillful edges I shall never
Find upon my own. The early sun
Defines the sea, the rough-shelled sand, clover
And cliff, as an instructor in Man-
As-Mathematics might rig a sum
Or two for me, proving that I could solve
In numbers what in love I'd overdraw, involve.

See how those rocks, toy boulders
Piled against Europe's ocean there, defend his land?
Now before school the young lord may stalk down
Pail-armed, from his father's sleeping shoulder
To forge his road, build his own castle, plan
Armadas. Yet see, in this winter dawn
Where the rocks end, small waves curve the sand
And there, fortressed by toadstools only, the grasses bend.

AT CHILMARK POND

At Chilmark Pond a cove of fog
hallows July this afternoon

pale skiff at rest
my history bears
softly: blurred grasses, disappearing dune.

The shreds of nightstorm,
lasering sun,
torment and first release, noon rain

in this found haven over Abel's Hill
exist not, all horizons gone.

Elizabeth Islands

The black rocks of Cuttyhunk
are diamond in the sun

The pale hills of Naushon
with sheep are overrun

Nonamesset, Pasque
and Nashawena gleam

beyond my sails in blue July,
the islands of a dream.

Some night in August
when harbors are asleep

I'll sail across to Naushon
and count the maze of sheep

and if, when startled cocks crow
the wind for home has died

I'll dig the deep blue mussels
from the morning tide.

Pitchdark.
The saltworks beach at Seven Gates
looms in my headlights: end of the pitted road.
Guilty of plotting trespass,
the site sacred beyond my noon imaginings
and not believing I would dare arrive,
I flip off my lights, sure the bass
will recognize me and retreat.

Thoreau once sensed, some fish all their lives
and never sense the fish are not the quest.
Nor are they mine, exactly, though tonight
I cannot guess what is: mysterious
connection with the night, the deep, the shore
I've come to uninvited. "Flyrods," my muse
has whispered, "unreel the most direct
lifelines to the soul."

Glass afternoons
I have watched
those islanders I long to understand
cast from the pier or jetty
or skim by in little boats,
stand still, send a costly filament
into the bluebottle air as if to catch
a roseate tern, an osprey gliding home.
The line would make a rainbow, descending as
it did against the sun—holding,
till the sea-patch darkened, spurted upward,
spewing a pewter flash, a luminous child's rocket,
caught, or disappearing downward, pearly grace and gone.

At midnight once I saw three pillared
silhouettes of gods, at sand's edge, working
the tide. The slim moon rose without a star
to guide it. Over the blackness—meadow,
current, sky—only the lifelines
gleaming, caught me, and the firefly
on the wave. Aeons earlier it seemed
I'd cast, myself, from major crafts
on heavy lines, cold mornings. But that
was artifice, and though my wrist still feels

SEVEN GATES

the pull, my throat the rush it felt
facing my quarry—
alarm because I knew
I'd not release it, others watching—
largely I have forgotten.

Now the narrow five-plank pier
stretches into darkness—danger—
lightening a bit as I, breath held, tiptoe out.
The dark will be as daylight
if I stand here long enough, and listen
for the splash, somewhere below. Waiting
as if the meaning beneath a lover's
sadness, his distraction or opacity,
could in the coming moment be revealed.

Silence. Shadows. Something else is missing.
Hope fails my long, slack line.
Is it the fireflies,
come with their offspring one by one
to the black scrub thickets
on the duney hillside now, flashing
tiaras at the sky's rim?
Perhaps they have been absent all these seasons
because I caught so many
artlessly on our childhood lawn,
believing the alchemy of their flame
must mean they loved my catching them,
that they'd found me.
Perhaps they have returned, trusting me
not to close them in a jar.

Who is it that can trust himself
the landscapes of temptation now so changed?

The line bends lightly first, sudden, strong. I pull
gently and then hard the other
player to my dominating hand.
Will I be able to release him from my hook
to mark exactly how that platinum streak
finds farther depths, that he might
find me, afterwards,
north at the sea's spire?

Long Point

A mile and a half
    along South Beach
as far as my summer
    eye can reach
the sand is iced
    with colored shells
shiny as Easter
    hushed as bells

are hushed this morning.
    The island sleeps,
all but one
    who a calendar keeps
and, rising early,
    blows out the moon.
Someone is humming
    a birthday tune.

Zack's

The lure of South Beach
      on a beautiful day
the crest of September
snow kingdom's December
blue windward and leeward in May

the lure that the curlew
      and sanderling know
of wildness and bluster
of limbo and luster
sun chasing the tail of the blow

when life is intense
      or contentious in town
too calm at the harbor
too rich by the arbor
the lawn in this heat turning brown

the lure like a rainbow
      He claimed there should be
stormcast to tease us,
catches us, frees us—
Come, Love, let us race to the sea!

Black Point

South Beach today

all blues and shimmering gray

like Danish porcelain

magnets my senses. I

choose opalescence, shell

secrets only mermaids tell.

And wild white swans

astonish the sky.

THE CLIFFS AT WINDY GATES

High fog: the sky is going,
the cliffs at Windy Gates
hang in an august dawn.

Mysterious as monks minding Tibet
we descend, unseen unseeing
each breath counted
all the way down.

Flatness reassures
our soles, the damp
grained sand.
Boundaries:
precarious clay wall
and petticoat sea.
This great lost beach
trusted once more is ours.

Now, centaurs and their quirk
reflections in the surf
come over the far sands
pounding, pounding.

At the sea's edge
sun-sensed we stand
arms wider for the wind
the clearing sky
to welcome those familiar creatures
man-and-beast, skewed mirrors
gone in the stillness of low tide.

SAND MUSIC

Falling asleep
on the beach in September,
the last ferry's oboe gone,
I am caught in the cobwebs
of dusk in the hammock
of wickets that sprouted
croquet on the lawn,
of lattices climbing
with trumpets and moonseed
and clouds in their haloes
at dawn.

F i n d i n g   A g a i n

FINDING AGAIN THE SECRET TREE-DARK PATH
FROM HEROES AND THE WORLD OF ORDER HIDDEN,
TRACING ITS LEAFY ARCS, THE PUNGENT ARBORS,
THE REDSTART BEAKS NIBBLING AT DAYBREAK'S SILENCE,

CLIMBING THE ROCKY STEPS NOW FAR FROM HARBORS
WE QUICKEN, CAUGHT IN MIDSUMMER TORRENTS
OF OLD ANTICIPATION. THE OPENING — SKY
THROUGH PALE VENETIAN PRISMS DAZZLES THE GRASS

AGAIN, BEYOND THE LAND DAZZLES THE OCEAN.
BUT, FOOTFAULT. THE CLIFF-EDGE — JAGGED SUDDEN
CLEFT BY OUR RECENT WINTERS OF EROSION
THE GOLD MAPPED BEACH DOWN THERE, NO STAIRS, NO PASS

YET CHILDHOOD'S BRINK HERE OFFERED TO MADDEN.

STAY? RETRIEVE THE DARK? TAKE HEROES' MEASURE?
THREE TIDAL KNIGHTS HAIL US AND CANTER BY.
"HURRY," THEY CALL, "LEAP DOWN! WE'RE OFF FOR TREASURE!"
SUCH WILD CHOICE RAVELS MORNING, FORBIDDEN.

THE FOG BLOWS BY

The fog blows by
returns, seeking Squibnocket's dune
obscures the sky
pond grass rocks shoreline and soon
the last of summer
friends climbing the steep chalk sand.

Imagining sunset in the wilderness
as one they stand
till dark.
Then something hovers, beats,
takes wing.
High-balanced, Tess and Rosey part
veil after veil of air

while Constance leaves for love's adventuring,
and Lucy's gone to cut her summer hair.

Beach Walk

I'm older than these spiky cliffs
and older than the sea,
walking the silent sunrise beach
there's no one old as me

no one to think of deaths to come
nor watch our footsteps fading
fast in the sands of morningtide
where the wind and I go wading.

99

MIDDLE ROAD

The double line
from Chilmark winding
leads me where
I cannot say
I love you
down the pitch of road
the steeper tide
this green and empty day.

SUNRISE ON SQUIBNOCKET POND

Sunrise on Squibnocket Pond
September out to sea:
a fleet of pirates—parchment swans—
sail to the edge where summer's gone
in fierce array
hold fall at bay
one morning more for Lucy, me.

Slant rays seek a roseate tern,
brilliant we glide from shore
across the silence swift and clear
as friendship or tomorrow. Near
blue herons dream
the dunes between
parting and here.

MENEMSHA

Scarlet sunset at Menemsha
sailors, fishermen all home
their craft and armor anchored
where we lie
watching a light wind's afterthought
stir the September harbor
masts gently joust
the deepening evening sky.

OAK BLUFFS

IN SUMMER THERE'S A MAGIC TOWN

(THE TOWN WHERE I WAS BORN)

WE VISIT WHEN THE SUN GOES DOWN

A MAGIC, MARVELOUS NIGHTTIME TOWN

WHERE A HUNDRED FACES ARE THE FACE OF A CLOWN

AND A HUNDRED SOUNDS A HORN

A HORN THE PIPER MUST HAVE PLAYED

IN HAMLIN LONG AGO

WHILE MOTHERS WATCHED THEIR CHILDREN FADE

DOWN COBBLED ALLEYS, UNAFRAID—

THESE ARE THEIR KINSMEN, ON PARADE

IN THE MAGIC TOWN I KNOW

WHERE CHINESE LANTERNS LIGHT THE TIDE
TO STREETS WHERE SWEETS ARE SOLD,
BRIGHT MUSIC BLARES AND PINBALLS SLIDE
AND LACE-TRIMMED HOUSES GLOW INSIDE
AND I ON THE FLYING HORSES RIDE
AND CATCH THE RING OF GOLD—

"OAK BLUFFS!" THE WINDS OF AUGUST CRY
"OAK BLUFFS!" THE SEAGULL CALLS.
WHEN DAY AT LAST HAS LEFT THE SKY
AND THE BEACH IS COLD, MY HEART CLIMBS HIGH
AND FOLLOWS THE WIND AND THE SEAGULL'S EYE
AND FAR WITH THE COMET FALLS.

ILLUMINATION NIGHT

The sky is dark
old lanterns glow
beneath the leaves
through cut-out porches
belfry, balconies,
bannister, eaves

The Oak Bluffs moon
captured, parcels
its orient beams
enchants us strolling
one last hour
free as our dreams

WHITENESS

Every April when our plum tree
spreads its wings in wedding bloom
I am again obsessed by whiteness—
whiteness, rhyme, and Rome.
But April's over the hill this year,
and I have promised not to rhyme,
and Rome where love began again so often
is abandoned.

Whiteness remains: obsessions: tall
sails rounding East Chop harbor,
cloud flotillas through my kites,
swans racketing above the dunes,
bleached alligator skeleton and
paper butterfly washed up from the
Okavanga on the long white
breakers that devour my shore.

Or, summer slipped away: a wide
verandah rocking to Virginia,
white pillars holding up the James,
Polly's commencement dress fluttering
in the attic storeroom whose window
will not close this autumn, strands
of a memoried grandmother's
unpinned hair. Even
the ice that held our skateblades up
is disappearing under snow,
knobbed white-stocking birches
our replacement.

Tomorrow, what shall I do
with whiteness? What is there about
mortality, immortality, when great
white birds take wing? Memory walks
a Himalayan ridge, between high
spaces, old friend standing
on the last field-edge behind me
counting disappearing yaks,
old friend striding oblivious ahead
toward Nirvana, each of us balancing his own
present destiny

in Bhutan's white kingdom,
Buddha's tiger waiting
at the monastery, snow falling,
falling, white and unseen cranes
asleep below.

To waste these days! The wind
still shimmering each high bouquet,
—these nights! The Milky Way,
old Pegasus who dives outside my
window, scattering moonlit seeds
white on the farthest wave.
Sheer curtains billow, but I cannot
close the casement on such fantasy.

Concert at the Tabernacle

Laemmergeyer gliding
the high Rift Valley
small plane humming
where Manyara gleams
herds of wildebeest
below us roaming
reel in
our flight of dreams.

Green leaves feather
the Tabernacle
the sun keeps time
as the music flames
angels are tilting
to a blue guitar
this Sunday in September
our enchantment: James.

TASHMOO FARM

Mist curtain rising at Tashmoo farm:

black fence, black trees emerge as gray,

black horses sweep their chestnut tails

across the watered sky, welcoming day.

Alert the bright-winged harrowed fields,

green hilly pastures wildflower-starred,

the berry trails, the sun-gemmed lake:

daughters on steeds, by Nature charged

will soon be fiercely trotting through

each of their summer provinces to guard.

CAPE POGUE

When I am old as Socrates
and suns have bleached my mind
with herring gulls I'll sail and dive
this golden Vineyard strand.
Starlight will comb the looking glass
all glittering days behind
as I follow silver minnows
into wonderland.

A Vineyard place
of undeciphered signs. The road stands still,
widens among the flints and copper ferns
and climbs
a grass-abandoned hill.

Oakleaves rustle underfoot, charged,
wary of rain.
November's sun, sly laser, streaks a field
drowsing to Indian glory as if done
with the nourishment of grain.

INDIAN HILL

Savannah sparrows in the empty furrow play
hopscotch, a southern tune.
Red squirrels from my childhood leap the air.
A crow is king in the peeling sycamore.
The clarion loon

turns every wind-belled charm
toward golden dangers:
a fall from limbs of grace, release, be found
as leaves brighter than autumn jewelry floating
the walls sands buoys of Vineyard Sound.

I have been afraid to lose my way, desire
magic of summer, the extending light,
afraid of scholarship's intensity
staring alone
down every traitor height.

Or poised to follow where the snow moon sailed
I'd court its misty brilliance till the true
moon stared back, beckoned. Then I'd deny
the night's wit and the stars'
laughter, the sweet tide. Rue, rue.

Sunset will come, and winter
but through the always anguished-and-too-early
dark I sense they scheme
to haunt no longer all my Chilmark
sanctuaries, only illuminate

those manuscripts, this harvest, buried dream.

The
Sunday Bells

The Sunday bells from island towns
chime down the harbor, up the lanes
where you and I
abed still lie
humming the night's romantic tunes.

White spires that pierce those royal skies
prick not our consciences nor tease
our common hearts
when summer charts
celestial Vineyard days.

VINEYARD ELEGY

Once, before the sun went down
I saw three gulls at Edgartown

wheeling, wheeling round a mast
empty of sails. As if time past

had come again, as if this harbor
greening wild, bloomed as an arbor

still: no lighthouse, no sure dock
or perfect dwellings, only hillock
and vines tumbling with grape and plum,
and myriad sands—he too had come
this tired sailor, under his mast
stretched out dreaming. His eyes, cast

upward to gauge the gulls' courage
a world ago, before his voyage

was over and lost and won,
are furled with the sun.

BALLAD OF MARTHA'S VINEYARD

My island in the morning
is the palest porcelain sky
a gull call and a whistle
and the ferry gliding by

clematis spilling on the hedge
and children on the pier
and sounds of summer everywhere
I turn again to hear.

My island in the morning
is blue enameled sky
clouds that hide a thousand kites
and sailboats slanting by

grasses to rouse my early feet
shells to rule the sands
and miles of crystal mirroring
the long-bright lands

'til fountains, far Ravello,
ruined temples on the Nile,
old libraries—Isla Negra's—
or Zanzibars beguile

and labyrinth and white fjord
volcano, cave, and cay
and spice routes to the Orient
set spinnakers for me.

Returning with the morning
a pomegranate sky
the bay a pewter symphony
as geese go honking by

and mica panes that glisten
from houses on the beach,
the lighthouse like an Indian scout
measuring autumn's reach,

I sight a Vineyard harbor,
a foil and tissue sky,
the echo of a foghorn,
an airplane silvering by,

a sea of opals breaking,
a moonshell opening wide,
and fishermen gone seeking
where the lucks of winter ride—

O, stay as morning, Island,
a changing song and sky
a lover, a deceiver
while my life goes skimming by

in stormclouds and a racer's wind,
fresh rain and spits of foam,
the bay a sudden topaz
and a rowboat coming home.

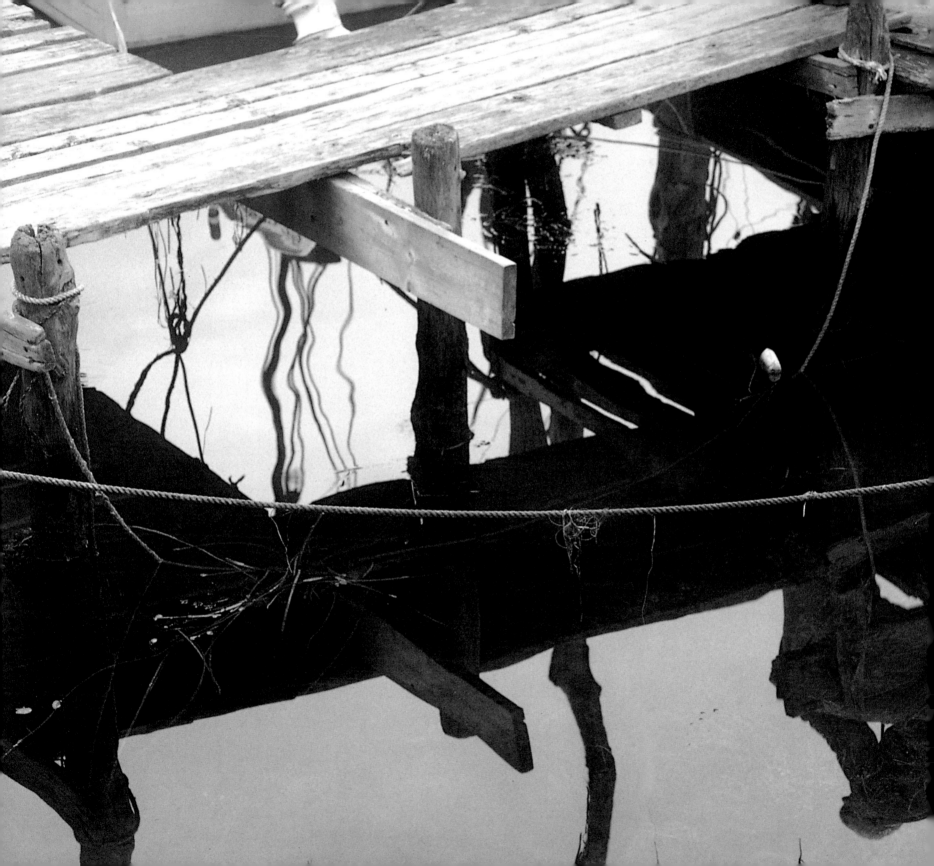

PHOTOGRAPH CAPTIONS